YAH AND HIS MESSENGER

BEHIND THE SCENES: A CRASH COURSE TO HIS CHURCH

ROSE E. MURPHY

Front Cover Image by Beyond The Book Media LLC

Book Design by Beyond The Book Media LLC

ISBN 978-1-7342566-5-9

CONTENTS

This journal of writings I dedicated with love to my Mother Mable Murphy and her late siblings, Thomas Lynn, Catherine, Retha Mae, Dorothy, Mary Elizabeth, and Johnnie, the children of the late Thomas William and Clara Murphy. We honor the late Isabelle Anderson Murphy and husband, Henry Murphy. We pay homage to their children, Thomas William, Bertha, Ida Ann, Rena, Geneva, John Henry, Inez, Nora, and Henry, a small fraction of their descendants: the sons and daughters of Yah's remaining remnant the children of Jacob, the seed of Abraham.

ACKNOWLEDGMENTS

I want to thank all the sons and daughters of the Most High who carry a mantle of a Prophet for their obedience to join the race in setting the captives free. It was the Prophetic inspirational writings of Mary Clark that caught my attention online more than twenty years ago. It was Mary Clark Chosen by God as his team organizer in connecting prophets, through her prophetic writings to the Church. Mary, who I consider a pillar in the heart of God, came in my life via the information superhighway at precisely the right time with her love letters from the Lord. Mary, whom I genuinely appreciate and am very thankful she linked me to the writings of Marsha Burns. Chosen by God (Yah), Marsha answered his call faithfully, always giving God the Glory. I especially would like to recognize Marsha Burns with her husband Bill, who I observed for two decades, navigate thousands of Eagles through the realm of the spirit. Marsha, through the anointing of the Holy Spirit with her daily fresh Manna from Heaven, saved thousands of lives. Marsha gave the earthly solution from the Lord for all our obstacles ahead through the realm of the spirit. When I was getting slaughtered spiritually, she made the calls for a course correction on my earthly realm. God (Yahuah) could not have chosen a better couple to shepherd his new harvest of souls entering into his Kingdom here on earth. I also would like to give thanks to Glenn Jackson, who delivered a confirmation message many years ago that I was here to bless others, which kept me grounded in my calling. I thank the Lord that Glen, through his prophetic writings, teachings, and observance of the word of God, continues to instruct the Body of Christ in this last leg of the race for the Prize the High Calling. Glen, through the anointing of the Holy Spirit, teaches the Church to live righteously and become Holy Vessels for the New Glorious Church in the Kingdom of God.

These true Shepherds behind the scenes with a multitude of prophets have helped prepare the way of the Lord and made his path straight. In their commitment as prophetic scribes, they were able to reach the masses, the Bride of Christ, and his true Remnant, to connect spiritually to the Father to inherit the promise.

Special thanks to Chanel Martin, the Lord's millennial marketplace Prophet, who he has Chosen because of her dedication and obedience to remove the chains of bondage from his people to enter into their callings as a new generation of prophetic scribes. (Isaiah 58 King James Version).

Thank You

Peace and Blessings

Love, Sister Rose

THE INVITATION

W hen Yah has a plan, it is a biblical fact that he always fulfills his design! He made a covenant promise to his people that they would inherit the Kingdom of Yah (God). The Lord God of Israel has prepared a strategy to make good on that promise. The youngest to the oldest, richest to the poorest from all nations, will inherit the Kingdom of Yah (God) because of their faithfulness to believe in his Son Yahusha Ha Mashiach, the Messiah (Jesus Christ), and walk-in righteousness and holiness. It's time for his people to get ready for this formal affair. When someone hosts a party, the guest prepares for the event and then attends. They are to come in the right attire and mannerism and show respect to the host. Yah (God) is the host of this gathering, and we are to show reverence to the Lord. As believers, by the unction of the Holy Spirit (The Comforter), we respond to the Spirit of Truth. Many of us have heard throughout the years coming from a pulpit somewhere in the world; the Holy Spirit is a perfect gentleman. The Lord does have manners, and everything he speaks to his people is always for their edification, even in correction.

11 For I know the thoughts that I think toward you, saith the Lord, thoughts of peace, and not of evil, to give you an expected end. (Jeremiah 29:11 King James Version)

The Lord does not want you to attend this event and not show you the preparation process for attendance. It's an invitation, and he will not force anyone to be present. However, he can stop your entrance to attend if you are not prepared. To participate in this affair, change has to come. Yah (God) is giving specific Ministers instructions to assist his people to prepare them for his party. Many are called, but few are chosen for this affair. (Matthew 22: 1-14 King James Version)

Anyone who throws a party can start with a small guest list. Then the numbers increase until you put a limit on the capacity. The Lord has no limit when it comes to souls for his Kingdom. Always remember the objective is souls for his Kingdom, and it does not change. We are a chosen generation, a royal priesthood statement, which means you are in the right place at the right time. The chosen generation makes you entitled to receive the benefits of this particular season in time.

9 But ye are a chosen generation, a royal priesthood, a holy nation, a peculiar people; that ye should shew forth the praises of him who hath called you out of darkness into his marvelous light; (1 Peter 2:9 King James Version)

It makes you eligible as heirs to enter into his Kingdom, prosper, be in health, and walk in the Glory of our Lord!

You will have to "war" in the Spirit to be a beneficiary and enter into the Kingdom of God to take hold of this trust fund! Worship will be your warfare! Many of God's children are unskilled for spiritual warfare. Some are considered babes in Christ. (Hebrews 5:13 King James Version)

It does not make them ineligible to enter the race for the Kingdom. It is not about warfare accomplishments. Instructions are so simple that our youth and a person with little or no education can follow.

Children of Yah (God), if we are walking in our flesh, we can't receive the benefits of his Kingdom! The deceptions and ungodly living that the Church got away with before will not enter into the Kingdom of Yah

(God) here on earth! Many people have repented received Christ for the remission of sins, who are baptized in the Holy Spirit of God and have left lifestyles of sin behind to move forward through this supernatural realm. They have also left the darkness of this world behind. The Lord requires his people to walk in righteousness and holiness without wavering.

15 For without are dogs, and sorcerers, and whoremongers, and murderers, and idolaters, and whosoever loveth and maketh a lie. (Revelation 22:15 King James Version)

9 Know ye not that the unrighteous shall not inherit the Kingdom of God? Be not deceived: neither fornicators, nor idolaters, nor adulterers, nor effeminate, nor abusers of themselves with mankind, 10 Nor thieves, nor covetous, nor drunkards, nor revilers, nor extortioners, shall inherit the Kingdom of God. (1 Corinthians 6:9-10 King James Version)

The Church is thirsty. The days of a little water to quench the thirst are almost over. The days of hunger for more of God are almost over. Because we know better, we will do better. As the sons and daughters of Yah (God) we are going to prepare to offer the Lord God of Israel our best offering, with the washing of the word, A Bride (A New Glorious Church) made without spot or blemish holy and without fault.

26 That he might sanctify and cleanse it with the washing of water by the word, 27 That he might present it to himself a glorious church, not having spot, or wrinkle, or any such thing; but that it should be holy and without blemish. (Ephesians 5:26-27 King James Version)

Sons and daughters of Yah (God) allow the gifting of the Holy Spirit of Yah (God) to flow freely in this move of the Lord, and many will evade the fires of hell for your obedience to prepare! (2 Timothy 1:6-7 King James Version)

It is your brothers and sisters in Christ that you help in this season. Some might say I go to Church, how do I help? In your sacrifice of preparation to walk in faith and not fear, it will cause an overflow into the Kingdom of Yah (God). The Lord's obedient ones will help to wake up his Church and tell them to get ready, "For the Kingdom of Yah (God) has come!" (Revelation 3:11-22 King James Version)

By faith, you have repented of your sins and redeemed by Christ, our Lord, and Savior. When you accept by faith the belief that Christ died for the redemption of your sins as Savior, it does not mean you live life according to all the morals of Yah (The Most High)! A lesson of selflessness, it will take to overcome all the wiles of Satan! It is time for you to operate in Yah's power, and you will need to walk in his stature.

The Lord God of Israel is pure and perfect. Now you will begin to prepare and become equipped for what is ahead.

If we adhered and represented righteousness truthfully for Yah (God), we would not have principles that lead us in his word on how to live a holy life. Putting on the whole Armor of God directs us to wear holiness daily that we may be able to stand against the wiles of the devil. (Ephesians 6:11 King James Version)

We do not wear our armor all the time. We are constantly bombarded by demonic forces not to comply with the directions of the Lord. We sometimes go forward without following or asking for directions. We as humans don't always accept instructions because our emotions (soul) and flesh (body) prefer to go against the Most High's nature (spiritual being) and reflections of his character.

So God created man in his own image, in the image of God created he him; male and female created he them. (Genesis 1:27 King James Version)

The battlefield in your soul (mind) tempts you to do what's not right.

Watch and pray, that ye enter not into temptation: the Spirit indeed is willing, but the flesh is weak. (Matthew 26:41, Romans 7:15-20 King James Version)

I can do all things through Christ, which strengthens me. (Philippians 4:13 King James Version)

23 For all have sinned and come short of the glory of God; being justified freely by his grace through the redemption that is in Christ Jesus: (Romans 3:23-24 King James Version)

As God's chosen people who are holy and loved, we are to keep our integrity and capture the characteristics of Yah (God) in our daily walk.

12 Put on, therefore, as the elect of God, holy and beloved, bowels of mercies, kindness, humbleness of mind, meekness, longsuffering (Colossians 3:12 King James Version)

In this preparation, the Lord wants his people to repent and forgive those who have hurt them physically and mentally.

14 For if ye forgive men their trespasses, your heavenly Father will also forgive you: 15 But if ye forgive not men their trespasses, neither will your Father forgive your trespasses. (Matthew 6:14-15 King James Version)

Once you repent and ask Christ into your heart, a transformation begins in your life of being born again.

3 Jesus answered, Verily, verily, I say unto thee, Except a man be born of water and of the Spirit, he cannot enter into the Kingdom of God. (John 3:5, Romans 12:1-3 King James Version)

If you have fallen out of the will of God, I have good news. It's the Grace of a Sovereign King who welcomes you again to enter into his presence and begin your journey into the Kingdom that is within you.

20 And when he was demanded of the Pharisees when the Kingdom of God should come, he answered them and said, The Kingdom of God cometh not with observation: 21 Neither shall they say, Lo here! Or lo there! for, behold, the Kingdom of God is within you. (Luke 17:20-21 King James Version)

The Lord never stops calling us from within our Spirit. He's in the Father, and you are in him, and he is in you.

20 At that day ye shall know that I am in my Father, and ye in me, and I in you. (John 14:20 King James Version)

23 I in them, and thou in me, that they may be made perfect in one; and that the world may know that thou hast sent me, and hast loved them, as thou hast loved me. (John 17:23 King James Version)

We are one body with many members. Our Lord is carrying the body of Christ, making intercession to save us and now bring the flock into the presence of Yah (God).

12 For as the body is one and hath many members, and all the members of that one body, being many, are one body: so also is Christ. 13 For by one Spirit are we all baptized into one body, whether we be Jews or Gentiles, whether we be bond or free; and have been all made to drink into one Spirit. 14 For the body is not one member, but many. (1 Corinthians 12:12-27 King James Version)

25 Wherefore he is able also to save them to the uttermost that come unto God by him, seeing he ever liveth to make intercession for them. (Hebrews 7:25 King James Version)

18 And Jesus came and spake unto them, saying, All power is given unto me in heaven and in earth. 19 Go ye therefore, and teach all nations, baptizing them in the name of the Father, and of the Son, and of the Holy Ghost: 20 Teaching them to observe all things whatsoever I have commanded you: and, lo, I am with you always, even unto the end of the world. Amen. (Matthew 28:18-20 King James Version)

If you don't have the baptism of the Holy Spirit to start your journey in Christ, it can be a big battle holding onto salvation and not falling back into sin and bondage. I'm not saying you can't backslide with the anointing of the Holy Spirit because you can fall, but you have direct access to the Father (God) in heaven, and the Holy Spirit makes intercession for you! (Acts 2:4, Mark 16:17 King James Version)

Having the baptism of the Holy Spirit helps to level you up in power and promotions in Yah (God). Once you receive the Holy Spirit, you are not a Babe in Christ, but in training to be seasoned in your calling from God. Benefits include direct communication to The Most High Yah (God)!

1 And I, brethren, could not speak unto you as unto spiritual, but as unto carnal, even as unto babes in Christ. 2 I have fed you with milk, and not with meat: for hitherto ye were not able to bear it, neither yet now are ye able. (1 Corinthians 3:1-2 King James Version)

The enemy waits to steal the word of God as soon it's, sown in your Spirit.

15 And these are they by the wayside, where the word is sown; but when they have heard, Satan cometh immediately, and taketh away the word that was sown in their hearts. (Mark 4:15 King James Version)

Now that you have received the Holy Spirit who makes intercession for you, the enemy has more of a battle to adapt too because your giftings are increasing. (1 Corinthians 14 King James Version)

People of God, you will not win against the enemy without an anointing from God. It's our call from the Most High to teach and pray for his sheep, who have no anointing or are not skilled to fight! The Lord is calling us to give proper instruction, and then his people can overcome the flesh and the wiles of the devil! We are all human and are not without sin. (Isaiah 10:27 King James Version)

Although we will be preparing a people to enter from Church age to Kingdom age and that small window of opportunity is crucial in this hour! Strait is the gate, and narrow is the way which leads to life, and few there be that find it. (Matthew 7:14 King James Version)

Church, this is not a calling that should be taken lightly. You are to become the vessels Yah will use to walk in his Power and Glory to bring his Spirit into the earth! The Lord has an Army of Prophets in the realm of the Spirit fighting for you until you come through your season of preparedness. It's not just to create wealth and to do the miraculous but to allow God to use your temple so he can flow through you and destroy wickedness from the face of the earth!

THE GLORY OF THE LORD CAN'T BE CONTAINED. IT IS SO RADIANT AND POWERFUL. THE AMOUNT OF GLORY THE LORD WANTS TO RELEASE A FEW CHOSEN ONES, CAN'T CONTAIN THE GLORY OF THE LORD. THAT MUCH GLORY AND POWER WOULD DESTROY A FEW PEOPLE. CHOSEN WARRIORS HAVE WARRED PREPARED THE PATH, AND NOW THE LORD WANTS HIS CHURCH TO PREPARE.

HIS CHOSEN WORSHIPPERS ARE IN THE DRIVERS SEAT READY TO LEAD YOU UP! HE SAID, IN THE LAST DAYS, HE WOULD POUR OUT HIS SPIRIT ON ALL FLESH.

17 And it shall come to pass in the last days, saith God, I will pour out of my Spirit upon all flesh: and your sons and your daughters shall prophesy, and your young men shall see visions, and your old men shall dream dreams: (Acts 2:17 King James Version)

29 And also upon the servants and upon the handmaids in those days will I pour out my Spirit. 30 And I will shew wonders in the heavens and in the earth, blood, and fire, and pillars of smoke. (Joel 2:29-30 King James Version)

I was listening to a beautiful testimony on the radio and ended it with Leukemia never goes into remission. This relative had so much love and faith to help their relatives through this illness. The relative ended her phone call, giving God the glory for his daily interventions to ease their loved one physical pain and stress. I pray all members of the body of Christ become skilled in this race towards the High Calling and arrest and destroy premature deaths in every realm of the Spirit as you move out onto this battlefield with the Lord in authority.

The voice of the Lord says, "You will have Power and Glory to destroy sickness," I will write your future and end. Straight is the gate and few find it! You, my people, want to be counted in that Chosen few that find it!"

I pray that those who accept Yah's (The Most High's) invite reply to the Lord with an RSVP by way of prayer, and thanks.

And he saith unto me, Write Blessed are they which are called unto the marriage supper of the Lamb. And he saith unto me these are the true sayings of God (Revelation 19:9 King James Version)

I am Sister Rose, Chosen One, the Lord's Messenger, from the Tribe of Judah. I am the Revelator. I go for his Namesake!

9 For my name's sake will I defer mine anger, and for my praise will I refrain for thee, that I cut thee not off. 10 Behold, I have refined thee, but not with silver; I have chosen thee in the furnace of affliction. 11 For mine own sake, even for mine own sake, will I do it: for how should my name be polluted? And I will not give my glory unto another. (Isaiah 48:9-11 King James Version)

8 Nevertheless, he saved them for his name's sake, that he might make his mighty power to be known. (Psalm 106:8 King James Version)

IGNITE THE FIRES (PROPHECY)

Let my armor-bearers go forth with my fires

It's time to ignite the fires

I said I would deliver my people

My word shall not come back void

The lost and the desolate

I shall deliver

I shall deliver the brokenhearted

Listen to my lead saith the Lord

I have waited long enough

I told my people to prepare for the harvest I said, get ready

for the harvest is about to come in Listen to my lead

saith the Lord I am igniting the fires

In order for my will to be done

Let my warfare go forth

I shall remove the darkness

the blind shall see

and the lame shall walk

those held captive shall be free

Listen to my Lead saith the Lord

Souls for my kingdom

That is my agenda

I shall not be moved

I shall not be hindered

Ignite the fires

I GIVE THEE UNDERSTANDING (PROPHECY)

I am not a spirit of confusion. I give thee understanding of the things to come. Satan has no authority in this place. I take all authority in this place. I am the God of Israel. I break into pieces the works of the wicked. I call forth my armor bearers to go forth with my fires.

My desire is to bring in my harvest. I shall not be moved. Shall I burn the chaff saith the Lord? I shall burn it with an unquenchable fire. My people fight battles, and they do it in the name of the Lord. The battles are fought to reduce the attacks against my people. I have many that stand in the gap for thousands. Then I have many who stand in the gap for the whole Body of Christ.

A price has been paid for Revelation Knowledge. Some have paid with their lives. It has cost some their families. I am about to recompense them for courage, and their love for me. For many have sacrificed many things. Many have sacrificed the luxuries of this world. Oh, how I love the sacrifice. Many of my people who would have been lost have been found, because I have Faithful Ones who have sacrificed much for me. I have your reward with me, Saith God!

I tell my people who I have Called, I have entrusted thee with much saith the Lord. You have been faithful in little, so I give thee much, saith God. You cried out for the souls of men. I shall send you my harvest my joy.

Oh, how I love the battle. A different type of warfare has been fought for my kingdom. My warriors run to battle in the spirit. I have stood by your side day and night. Oh, what a battle we have fought. You are strong and mighty in the Lord. You have been chosen for the battlefield to set the captives free. I have thy reward with me, saith God.

These shall make war with the Lamb, and the Lamb shall overcome them: for he is Lord of lords and King of kings: and they that are with him are called and chosen and faithful. (Revelation 17:14 King James Version) 31 But many that are first shall be last; and the last first. (Mark 10:31 King James Version)

17 And if ye call on the Father, who without respect of persons judgeth according to every man's work, pass the time of your sojourning here in fear: (1 Peter 1:17 King James Version)

HE IS THE ORCHESTRATOR

Many are preparing for the great outpouring of the Lord. As saints, we should have a desire to be ready for his coming. There is no time to waste, quarrel, or have a critical spirit and judge others. God is ready to manifest his presence, power, and glory in and around us. We have many different doctrines in the body of Christ that will hinder a lot of saints from receiving the full manifestation of God's power. The different doctrines do not mean Christians will perish and be lost in hellfire. It just means some will not be at the same level to receive this outpouring of God's spirit. His power and glory will be evident; however, many will miss the magnificence of his coming. The enemy is distracting God's sheep. Some saints have only grown as far as their church doors and lived under one teaching, and some, unfortunately, have been deceived under the doctrine of devils. Some saints are busy building resumes in God while he is building a kingdom. Man-made works will not set the captives free. It will only release a scattering of sheep. There is no power and glory in the flesh. Let us be mindful to pray that a change takes place in the spirit rapidly to prepare the saints for the blessing.

Souls for the Kingdom of God is the most important call Yah (God) is leading. A harvest that will need deliverance and healing is coming. The outpouring will cause the heavens to shake and the enemy to surrender all.

Those that say they are saved and are not will turn away. Just like in the word, some say they are Jews but are not. The sin of man will not be able to adapt to the glory of God. That will be the great falling away.

However, the new harvest will continue to come and be ready to receive all the Father is pouring out in these last days. God is separating the chaff from the wheat, the goats from the sheep. What is his and what is not. Saint's the Lord does not want us tossed to and fro. When they (the chaff) turn away from the Lord, do not follow them into their sin and rebellion. Remember, it is God doing the actual separating. God is the Orchestrator of his church.

For the Lord will not forsake his people for his great name's sake: because it hath pleased the Lord to make you, his people. (1 Samuel 12:22 King James Version)

THE OPPOSITION

For we wrestle not against flesh and blood, but against principalities, against powers, against the rulers of the darkness of this world, against spiritual wickedness in high places. (Ephesians 6:12 King James Version)

When marching through the realm of the spirit, darkness has to move out of your path. Every obstacle has to be removed and destroyed as you move toward the high calling. Every assignment from the enemy is waiting to fight you on this end-time call of God. This isn't a one-man show. It's teamwork.

The psalmist shall lead, the worshipper's worship, warriors shall war. Fires of song, fires of tongues, fires of his warfare, and the worship service should not end until the church receives a breakthrough. That means Yah's people throughout this earth should be in a continual mode of worship around the clock. If I'm sleeping, another son or daughter of the Most High will be worshipping for the body of Christ in another time zone. Yah's warriors are standing in the gap in worship and prayer, for the Body of Christ and the Lord God of Israel will supernaturally bring you into his presence at the appointed time simultaneously.

Most Saints have experienced a breakthrough in prayer. Now we will advance as a body of believers in unity. Sing, worship, and war your way into his presence, power, and glory. Hell shall bow at your coming.

9 Hell from beneath is moved for thee to meet thee at thy coming: it stirreth up the dead for thee, even all the chief ones of the earth; it hath raised up from their thrones all the kings of the nations (Isaiah 14:9 King James Version)

4 For the weapons of our warfare are not carnal, but mighty through God to the pulling down of strongholds; (2 Corinthians 10:4 King James Version)

The thief cometh not, but for to steal, and to kill, and to destroy: I am come that they might have life and that they might have it more abundantly. (John 10:10 King James Version)

28 And fear not them which kill the body, but are not able to kill the soul: but rather fear him which is able destroy both soul and body in hell. (Matthew 10:28 King James Version)

THE WAR PLAN (PROPHECY)

I bring forth my Bride without spot or blemish. I have not come to destroy my ministers and those that walk in other offices. I shall take them through the fires of my love saith the Lord. The spirit of division is among you. Discern it and get rid of it. I know the hearts of my people. I created you all for my Glory, honor, and purpose. Those who choose to march with me into battle will receive their reward. I am a life-giver, and my divine purpose and order will be fulfilled. Do not pick up the weapons of warfare of the enemy or his tools and devices. I have given each of you instructions, and they have not changed.

Worship is your warfare!

THE WAR PLAN

I t is the stronghold of wickedness that keeps people in bondage! The Lord will empower his people with his Power and Glory to fight! That's how the Lord will destroy wickedness, through you his chosen vessels. Sons and daughters of Yah (God), Chosen is not just a title you wear for show and do a sing-along. It's a call, an assignment from the Kingdom of heaven, to be a part of a Chosen Generation.

The Lord showed me his war plan. In the year 2000, the Lord said to me he would destroy wickedness from the four corners of the earth point to point! The Lord then showed me his world map in what appeared to be his control center. The highlighted red lines targeted each continent.

The wicked's walk is organized in spiritual realms and dedicated to their cause. They know each other in the spirit and operate under the influence of darkness and evil.

God uses all of his people according to skill and training in spiritual warfare! We wrestle (war) not against flesh and blood but skilled demonic forces of satan. The Lord does not want you to be afraid; he will fight as you rise in faith to believe and walk in revelation knowledge.

Demonic forces have one assignment from the enemy to keep you out of the realm of the spirit. Why are they working so hard to keep you out of those dominions? Did I mention your blessings are also in the spirit realm? The wicked of the earth have been enjoying many of the benefits of your entitlements. You believe in a supernatural God by faith. It's time to get off this natural realm of thinking and enter into spiritual realms where The Lord Jesus Christ (Yahusha Ha Mashiach) leads the battle with warring Angels and Chosen Warriors who run to the battle. It's time for the church to run to the fight.

13 There hath no temptation taken you, but such as is common to man: but God is faithful, who will not suffer you to be tempted above that ye are able; but will with the temptation also make a way to escape, that ye may be able to bear it. (1 Corinthians 10:13 King James Version)

I was taught by religion to believe a traditional way of thinking, such as pay your tithes, sow a seed to receive a blessing from the Lord.

While the earth remains, seedtime and harvest, cold and heat, summer, and winter, and day and night shall not cease. (Genesis 8:22 King James Version)

There is no reason you should not support your place of worship where the children of God (Yah) gather and fellowship. Churches and Camps have expenses to keep the doors open. Yahs leaders are responsible when it comes to his storehouse and those seeds planted. The church has helped many suffering people throughout the years all over the earth. No money tithe or offering is required to receive this blessing from the Lord. Just follow the God of Israel's instructions. We have the wicked spiritually high jacking our promises in the realm of the spirit, and the Lord is going to make sure the church does not take part in any more corruption knowingly. (John 10:1-10 King James Version)

I did not know anything about spiritual realms, beings, or have a belief in such things. Then one day on a train station platform, a young man walked up to me, handed me a pamphlet of graphic art with teachings about Jesus, spiritual beings, and the things we do not see with our natural eyes. It was the first seed sown to me on deliverance. I was 18 years old, and I was not born again! I shared the pamphlet with a gentleman from a religious organization that knocks on doors. I saw him a few months later, but the booklet I never saw again. Years later, through the power of the Holy Spirit, God (Yah) revealed to me that every word in that pamphlet was accurate.

18 While we look not at the things which are seen, but at the things which are not seen: for the things which are seen are temporal; but the things which are not seen are eternal. (2 Corinthians 4:18 King James Version)

POWER AND GLORY TO FIGHT (PROPHECY)

My power and Glory are to fight in the battle and destroy the onslaught of the enemy. I give you my power my anointing to destroy yokes and bondages and have freedom and liberty. I give you my Glory, not for show but to destroy everything in your path of darkness. To shine where there is no light. The enemy is using everything he has to throw you off course and hinder your destiny. I have come with revelation knowledge to direct your steps. My power and Glory are not for sale. I search the heart of man, and I see he has already made a sale. I cannot be bought or sold. A demonstration of my power and Glory are not for sale. There is nothing hidden from me saith the Lord. I told you for years to get ready, get ready for the harvest of souls. I have many who have a need for your service in the Lord. My vessels shall be used for my Glory and honor. I am here, and I have been here for a while. I have come to bless my people a blessing I shall not miss saith the Lord.

PROPHETIC PROCLAMATION (POETIC)

For the enemy would try to deceive thee in these last days Saith the Lord, thy God

But I say, not so

For I'll go far, I'll go wide

I'll go high, and I'll even go low

Saith the Lord thy God

To take back what belongs to me

It doesn't matter to me

if it's one or two

Saith the Lord

The fact of the matter is it's mine

And I tell you there are two types harvest

Saith the Lord thy God

The one that's about to scatter

And the one I'm about to reap

Saith the Lord

And my word never changes

It's the same yesterday

Today and forever

Saith God

Woe unto those Pastors

Who bruise and scatter my sheep

Saith the Lord

And I tell you it's not time to multiply

yet saith the Lord

For I am the one who adds and subtracts the sheep

And right now I am dividing the chaff from the wheat

What's mine, what's not

And I tell you the reason

There are so many attacks

Saith the Lord

Because you're in the middle of the battlefield Saith God

But I tell you me my people If you endure until the end Saith the Lord

I will give thee a crown of GLORY!

Saith the Lord thy God

REPENTANCE

M any denominations in the Church of Christ follow different doctrines with other views on repentance. The message to repent daily has slightly gone over the Church's head. Some people confess their sins daily and many not at all. Repentance should come day by day because we live in a sinful world and are trying to communicate with a Holy God that cannot touch sin. He has a plan to heal the nations. We sin daily, in our actions, and many of us aren't aware that our daily words and thoughts do not line up with the will of Yah (God). It's time to examine ourselves and become accountable for what we say and do on this journey. Yah knows what you are thinking at all times. Just because you don't speak it out verbally does not disqualify it as a sin. If you speak a pleasant word to someone, yet your thoughts are not pleasant, then you lied to that person and thought evil in your mind (soul). Your body is the temple of the Holy Spirit, and our thoughts matter to the Lord (Yah). (Ephesians 4:29, Matthew 15:8 King James Version)

Let us pray as you begin your journey of deliverance to Destiny.

Yah God of Israel

I believe Christ died for the redemption of my sins. I receive him in my heart as my Lord and Savior. I ask you, Yah God of Israel (The Most High Creator of Heaven and Earth), to forgive me for my daily sins. I repent of known and unknown sins and anything not pleasing to you, Lord. Create in me a clean heart and renew a right spirit in me, Lord. I petition you with a pure heart. Yah, help me to do your will for your glory and honor. Lord, I will repent daily and continually stay in your presence through prayer, worship, and your word. I will think about these things what is true, honest, just, pure, lovely, whatever things are of good report praiseworthy and have any virtue. (Philippians 4:8 King James Version)

Yah, I understand you cannot touch sin because you are pure and Holy. Lord, teach me to be holy. Baptize me with your Holy Spirit. Lord, Yah, I understand that you are seeking empty vessels to pour your Power and Glory inside of without spot or blemish, and my body is the Temple of the Holy Spirit! I accept your call with thanksgiving. Yah, I will follow your lead every day, any time of the day.

5 Casting down imaginations, and every high thing that exalteth itself against the knowledge of God, and bringing into captivity every thought to the obedience of Christ; (2 Corinthians 10:5 King James Version)

I will repent daily. I will not fight the Church and give the enemy any power against the Body of Christ. Worship is my warfare that will destroy the yoke bondages of Satan and set the captives free.

In the Name of the Yahusha Ha Mashiach (The Lord Jesus Christ), I give you all the Glory and Praise. So be it (Amen)!

People of God without Christ (The Messiah), the Son of God, you have no bridge to Yah (God). Many people have come into the Church and left because of unanswered prayers and many disappointments. Imagine finding Christ in 2019, feeling joyful of this new relationship with the Savior. Imagine new believers, delivered set free of bondage's, and the first message they hear is the Church needs to repent. That can become very confusing for a new believer. If they are around salty Christians (believers), it just drains the faith quickly because the enemy is right there to rob the word from a new saint (Brother or Sister) in Christ Jesus

(Yahusha Ha Mashiach). Do not teach new believers to hold grudges against others in the body of Christ. If you have an offense, repent and forgive. Family of Yah (God), this season, you will have to forgive those who sin against you to get through this realm. (Luke 17:1-4 King James Version)

12 Put on, therefore, as the elect of God, holy and beloved, bowels of mercies, kindness, humbleness of mind, meekness, longsuffering; 13 Forbearing one another, and forgiving one another, if any man have a quarrel against any: even as Christ forgave you, so also do ye. 14 And above all these things put on charity, which is the bond of perfectness. (Colossians 3:12-14 King James Version)

The Lord (Yah) has been calling the Church to repentance for years. I can't say how many have repented, but I can say not enough because the Lord is still appealing to his people to repent. If the Bride were ready, the groom would have arrived, and the promises would be apparent in our earthly realm. We do not want new believers to fall back into the world of sin and wickedness because we fail to obey Yah. The Lord will not have this type of fate for his new harvest of souls. He wants uncorrupted shepherds that will lead his sheep in truth, knowledge, and understanding.

How then shall they call on him in whom they have not believed? How shall they believe in him of whom they have not heard? and how shall they hear without a preacher? (Romans 10:14 King James Version)

The Lord has raised a new generation of believers who will answer his call. The Lord referred to you as the brats are coming, an uncompromisable generation. Yah molded you in your youth to bring you into your inheritance and ready for his kingdom. While the Lord gave some of his most loved Prophets (male and female) a head start, more prophets are joining the race.

14 Turn, O backsliding children, saith the Lord; for I am married unto you: and I will take you one of a city, and two of a family, and I will bring you to Zion: 15 And I will give you pastors according to mine heart, which shall feed you with knowledge and understanding. 16 And it shall come to pass, when ye be multiplied and increased in the land, in those days, saith the Lord, they shall say no more, The ark of the

covenant of the Lord: neither shall it come to mind: neither shall they remember it; neither shall they visit it; neither shall that be done any more. (Jeremiah 3:14-16 King James Version)

And he shall go before him in the spirit and power of Elias, to turn the hearts of the fathers to the children, and the disobedient to the wisdom of the just; to make ready a people prepared for the Lord. (Luke 1:17 King James Version)

Many sons and daughters who have left the Church seeking all truth, are not penalized by God. Many are warranted by the Lord to start camps, build refuges, and grow food.

When a church becomes a platform of a routine with no results, then the children of the Most High should be on a mission to find the will of Yah (God) for their life. Let us repent of hindering others who choose to follow the Lord (Yah) in a different lifestyle outside of the Church.

Do not become offensive to your brothers and sisters; pray that the Lord give them wisdom and direction to lead his sheep into his perfect will. Don't give demonic forces any fuel to throw you off course by arguing and backbiting each other. Rebuke the stronghold of division at every turn. That dividing spirit builds a stronghold by collecting jealousy, envy, strife, and bitterness only to deter you from destiny.

We live in a dying world, and the only hope for the lost is Christ, the Son of God. Many of us believed Christ died for our sins and once saved, always saved.

Stay on daily repentance people of Yah (God) because once saved, people can still go to hell. Let us not make a mockery of our Lord and miss this move of God because of false teaching. Let us be like the five wise virgins who had oil in their lamps and the oil represents kingdom living. In that lamp are faith, the word of God, anointing's, holiness, righteousness and love for one another. Everything you need to enter into the kingdom is in that oil lamp. What were the other virgins doing in life, and they had no time to prepare for the groom? They were too consumed with the carnal things of this world.

6 For to be carnally minded is death, but to be spiritually minded is life and peace. 7 Because the carnal mind is enmity against God: for it is not subject to the law of God, neither indeed can be. 8 So then they that are in the flesh cannot please God. (Romans 8:6-8 King James Version)

1 Then shall the kingdom of heaven be likened unto ten virgins, which took their lamps, and went forth to meet the bridegroom?

2 And five of them were wise, and five were foolish.

3 They that were foolish took their lamps, and took no oil with them:

4 But the wise took oil in their vessels with their lamps.

5 While the bridegroom tarried, they all slumbered and slept.

6 And at midnight there was a cry made, Behold, the bridegroom cometh; go ye out to meet him.

7 Then all those virgins arose and trimmed their lamps.

8 And the foolish said unto the wise, Give us of your oil; for our lamps are gone out.

9 But the wise answered, saying, Not so; lest there be not enough for us and you: but go ye rather to them that sell, and buy for yourselves.

10 And while they went to buy, the bridegroom came; and they that were ready went in with him to the marriage: and the door was shut.

11 Afterward came also the other virgins, saying, Lord, Lord, open to us.

12 But he answered and said, Verily I say unto you, I know you not.

13 Watch therefore, for ye know neither the day nor the hour wherein the Son of man cometh. (Matthew 25:1-13 King James Version)

Can "saved" people go to hell and the lake of fire? It is the objective of satan to destroy all humans and take as many with him as possible into the lake of fire because he knows his time is short. (Revelation 12:12 King James Version)

He knows the lake of fire was created for him and his angels, and he wants to take Yah's creation of humanity into his eternal damnation. Repent and learn your opponents (demonic forces) tactics and devices. Silence every dispute by not allowing the enemy to disrupt your homes, churches, and camps.

23

If something were not at risk, then you would never have opposition, and the enemy would never attempt to fight you spiritually. Yah wants his creation, delivered from the grips of the enemy. Souls for the kingdom is the agenda.

5 But I will forewarn you whom ye shall fear: Fear him, which after he hath killed hath power to cast into hell; yea, I say unto you, Fear him. (Luke 12:5 King James Version)

The Lord wishes that who so ever believes in him should not perish but have eternal life. (John 3:15-17 King James Version)

We are under the dispensation of grace, Christ, who died for our sins. (Ephesians 3:2 King James Version)

While the Lord is calling his people to repent, let us pray that they will awaken and come back into his fold.

14 The backslider in heart shall be filled with his own ways: and a good man shall be satisfied from himself. (Proverbs 14:14 King James Version)

4 For it is impossible for those who were once enlightened, and have tasted of the heavenly gift, and were made partakers of the Holy Ghost, 5 And have tasted the good word of God, and the powers of the world to come, 6 If they shall fall away, to renew them again unto repentance; seeing they crucify to themselves the Son of God afresh, and put him to an open shame. (Hebrews 6:4-6 King James Version)

21 Not everyone that saith unto me, Lord, Lord, shall enter into the kingdom of heaven; but he that doeth the will of my Father which is in heaven. 22 Many will say to me in that day, Lord, Lord, have we not prophesied in thy name? and in thy name have cast out devils? and in thy name done many wonderful works? 23 And then will I profess unto them, I never knew you: depart from me, ye that work iniquity. (Matthew 7:21-23 King James Version)

The Church has to become a model for the new harvest. Your example of sanctification will deter sheep from falling away from the faith and will catalyst them into the Kingdom of God here on earth. The Lord is not going to trust his New Harvest of souls to a corrupted Church. People of Yah get ready for a New Glorious Church without spot or blemish, walking in holiness. (1 Peter 1:16, Ephesians 5:27 King James Version)

Sons and daughters, this is your destiny, and you will understand every detail of the importance of your call from Yah (God) by revelation knowledge. As you begin to enter into this new intimate relationship with Yah, your spiritual atmosphere will start to change.

Do not worry about being deceived. Pray and ask the Lord for the gift of discernment. You will need his gift on your journey. (1 Corinthians 12:10, Psalm 119:66 King James Version)

I can remember when the Lord first began revealing to me his revelation pertaining to God's Chosen twenty-two years ago. Imitators with partial revealings will not get you through the realm of the spirit and take you to your inheritance. Every word I write is anointed by Yah (God). If you follow the Lord's lead, you will not be satisfied today and thirsty tomorrow.

Pray using your freedom and liberty in Christ to choose and try every spirit. (1 John 4:1 King James Version)

Remember, everything derives from somewhere and, no one can birth what they never conceived. The Lord laid a foundation many years ago, and his warriors have worked and developed a no-fail war plan to bring the Bride of Christ (The Church) through the spirit realm. Some have chosen wickedness and build on this foundation and make it belong to them for the luxury of greed. Their plans to steal the Lord's Glory have failed, and now their work will be tried by fire. This was never about a blessing for a chosen few. It was about a selected few doing the warfare to bring the Church into their promise. A people of no compromise who can't be bought (bribed) with greed and the lusts of this world. (Proverbs 13:11, 15:27, 20:21 King James Version)

The Lord never said his people should not get paid a wage for preaching and teaching the gospel. The Lord has a problem with lying and manipulating to collect a salary and robbing his sheep. (1 Corinthians 9:13-14 King James Version)

9 For we are laborers together with God: ye are God's husbandry, ye are God's building. 10 According to the grace of God, which is given unto me, as a wise master builder, I have laid the foundation, and another buildeth thereon. But let every man take heed how he buildeth thereupon. 11 For other foundation can no man lay than that is laid, which is Jesus Christ. 12 Now if any man build upon this foundation, gold, silver, precious stones, wood, hay, stubble. 13 Every man's work shall be made manifest: for the day shall declare it, because it shall be revealed by fire; and the fire shall try every man's work of what sort it is. 14 If any man's work abides which he hath built thereupon, he shall receive a reward. (1 Corinthians 3:9-14 King James Version)

9 And let us not be weary in well doing: for in due season we shall reap if we faint not. 10 As we have therefore opportunity, let us do good unto all men, especially unto them who are of the household of faith. (Galatians 6:9-10 King James Version)

SONG OF DELIVERANCE (PROPHETIC)

I tell you, my people

I tell you, my people

I'm about to restore

Everything the enemy has stolen

I'm about to restore

Everything the locust and

canker have eaten

But you have to pick up your cross

and follow me

Many are called

But few are chosen

and you are the few

I have chosen

Saith the Lord

But you have to pick up your cross

and follow me

Who will partake

of the first fruits

of the harvest

But you have to pick up your cross

and follow me

Pick it up

Pick it up

and follow me

Saith the Lord

Throughout the years, the Church got pitched many curveballs. It's when a pitcher causes a baseball to deviate from a straight path, and it spins, causing the person holding the bat to miss hitting the ball. Many Saints have missed the full revelation because those who delivered the word threw a spin to the message because they just did not have the full knowledge of the revelation in its entirety.

The Lord is releasing his Holy Prophets and Holy Apostles to bring correction to his Shepherds and Leaders who have deviated from his course. The Lord wants the entire Body of Christ on the right path. An altered revelation just will never take you to the finish line of this race. On this last leg of the race, no one will be able to carry anyone through to the finish line. Only obedience will take you to the finish line.

Once you finish the race, you will no longer travel anymore in a myriad of circles seeking scientific healings, philosophical deliverances, and untouchable blessings. The Lord will equip you with his Power to lay hands and heal the sick and do the greater works.

The Lord said he wished that you prosper and be in health. (3 John: 1:2 King James Version)

Your days of spiritual starvation and earthly poverty are ending. The greater works will soon flow through you from Yah, the Father. (John 14:12 King James Version)

Children of God, one day you will walk in the demonstration of his Power and Glory, then you will turn toward your neighbor and say, this is like a dream.

1 When the Lord turned again the captivity of Zion, we were like them that dream. 2 Then was our mouth filled with laughter, and our tongue with singing: then said they among the heathen, The Lord hath done great things for them. 3 The Lord hath done great things for us; whereof we are glad. 4 Turn again our captivity, O Lord, as the streams in the south. 5 They that sow in tears shall reap in joy. 6 He that goeth forth and weepeth, bearing precious seed, shall doubtless come again with rejoicing, bringing his sheaves with him. (Psalm 126:1-6 King James Version)

DON'T FIGHT THE CHURCH, NO PUN INTENDED, BUT NO FRIENDLY FIRE

The Bride of Christ is exchanging her rags for her wedding garments. The Lord wants his Church prepared and ready to go, and they shall not break ranks. (Joel 2:7 King James version)

The objective never changes! Souls for his kingdom! We go down into the pits, trenches, and pull out his people. Some sheep will come willingly, and some will need divine intervention from Yah (The Lord)!

For I'll go far, I'll go wide. I'll go high I'll even go low Saith the Lord to take back what belongs to me. It doesn't matter to me if it's one or if it's two. Saith God, The fact of the matter it's mine.

Those Leaders who refuse to pick up their Cross will miss a wave of blessings, and the sheep left under them will scatter! The Lord will gather his new harvest into his kingdom under his obedient prepared shepherds from the youngest to the oldest he will pour out his spirit. (Acts 2:17 King James Version)

The more God's warriors take enemy lines in the spirit; it pushes demonic forces out of their spiritual campgrounds into the realm of the spirit, which means earthly realm invasion. If your house, camp, and church comes under attack, you will still have to learn by trial and error to combat demonic forces and walk in love and righteousness. If you fall, pick yourself up, repent, apologize if needed, keep marching, and worshipping toward your goal (destiny). Many people will begin to repent because they will want the demonic attacks to stop before they sit and die! I'm not referring to aliens coming from outer space doctrines. These demonic forces will feel like an invasion when your spiritual atmosphere changes abruptly. The only thing a demonic force wants is a willing vessel to sabotage your walk. Beware, spiritual wickedness rules in high places in the realms of the spirit and principalities, powers of darkness rule in our earthly realm. Rulers of darkness are murdering evil forces; it just destroys everywhere it lands. The wicked summon these spirits and employ them to do their dirty work. What's the payment a human sacrifice.

We have frontline soldiers of Yah (God) in the realm of the spirit warring against these forces. We need them out the way so the Lord can bring up his Church. Remember, worship is your warfare, repent daily, and cast down those imaginations that exalt itself against the knowledge of God and bring those thoughts into captivity unto the obedience of Christ. Saint's, you have more ability to control the way you think than you may have ever acknowledged. (Psalm 23:7 King James Version)

According to the world population clock, there are close to 7,770.000.000 billion people on this earth, and every eight seconds someone dies, versus every twelve seconds someone is born. All souls matter to Yah. Life and death is a spiritual war, where good versus evil and eternal life versus eternal damnation. Yah needs his people to operate in his Power and Glory to pull souls into his kingdom. Some will fall by the wayside, and they will perish. However, many will come into the light of his glory when you operate in revelation knowledge and follow the Lord's lead. (Isaiah 60:1 King James version)

Yah is giving you instructions to run your race effectively. Do not look for portals or any of the enemy's devices to move through realms. Relinquish all ties to modern-day Babylon and any darkness or evil thinking by continually casting down those imaginations. You can't have one foot in the world and another foot in the kingdom. The enemy will attack you at every turn to deter you from your course.

The wicked are in the realm of the spirit, but they are operating under demonic forces. They are mere men and women and even children who've become sacrificial offerings to Molech! (Leviticus 18:21, Deuteronomy 18:10 King James Version)

The Lord's servants who are in the realm of the spirit, can't afford to miss their targets!

Your target will always be principalities, powers, rulers of darkness, and spiritual wickedness in high places! However, the Lord leads you in the spirit of war; always follow him in obedience.

Pray for the leaders who are shepherds over Yah's sheep. The enemy will send a multitude of assignments out to hinder many in unbelief. The spirit of pride is running rampant in the realms. We all know what it is like when it comes to overtaking you on the battlefield of your mind. It's the feeling of being puffed up! The spirits of pride like to play games. Don't play with them at any cost! Cast it down! Burn it, fire it up with consuming fires, and send it back to hell. Pray with spiritual tongues of fire (spiritual language). Worship is your warfare! The need to feel superior will never get you through the realm of the spirit. Walk-in humility, because the spirit of pride is assigned to deter you from your promises.

The Lord will not use the saints who are walking in the spirit of pride. Yah (God) is calling his children, and with some, he's using a rod of correction. It's either his way or the enemy will devour many of his people! Our Creator disciplines with love, and sometimes it doesn't feel good. (Proverbs 6 King James Version)

Whatever the case might be, our Father is always trying to protect us from the enemy just as parents are to protect their children. Souls for the kingdom will always be the plan no matter what condition his people approach his throne! (Psalm 82:3, James 1:27, Proverbs 22:6, Proverbs 13:24 King James Version)

If you are warring in the spirit, demonic forces will scatter! Do they come back? Yes, they do, and some with a new approach.

They will look for any crack in your foundation (gossiping and lying, etc..) to hinder your race.

Don't judge Yah's people. Yah is a righteous judge. Which means you would have to judge righteously! He will not leave the people that are called by his name any excuse for not picking up their Cross and following him. He will call them for however long he decides before making any type of judgment! Only Yah (God) can search the heart of man. (Jeremiah 17:10 King James Version)

Let us not try to decide who is worthy or not to hear and receive the call of Yah (God). Everyone needs something from the Lord in these terrible times. Like warriors, we go into the pit, pull them out, and deliver them into all truth! (Psalm 103:4, Matthew 12:11 King James Version)

Whatever the Lord leads you to do, go forth and just make sure it's Yah. Try every spirit. (1 John 4:1 King James Version) By using your new anointing of discernment, the wolves will become more noticeable as the gifts of Yah (God) increase.

Do not become anxious or overwhelmed; the battle is the Lord's, and Jesus Christ (Yahusha Ha Mashiach) is slaying the wolves for you! (1 Samuel 17:47 King James Version)

If you meet spiritual opposition from a leader, then pray against all demonic forces surrounding them or whomever you are witnessing too! It's hard to receive when you've had a bug (enemy) in your ear for so long! Remember, the spirit of pride has built strongholds around many leaders; they are concerned if they go in this direction; they will lose their flock (finances). If they don't go, they will lose their flock anyway!

The strongholds are no different for you as you move forth onto the battlefield and begin to move into the realm of the spirit. The enemy is going to throw accusations, assumptions as barricades in front of you to throw you off course. Deceptive little spirits will be whispering in your ears and thoughts. These are spiritual roadblocks. They are annoying, and they will find a member of your flock to help deter you from the truth.

That's why worship is your warfare. You will have to take authority over these pesky little demonic forces. Whatever you do, don't allow these evil spirits to give you ammunition to shoot your brothers and sisters in Christ (Yahusha) down. If you don't agree, take everything to the Lord in prayer.

If you are skilled in warfare, then fight in the spirit for the body of Christ like you would for your family and those you know and love. The Lord will reward you for your service. (John 15:13 King James Version)

WORDS ARE POWER

A re not words Power? Words travel through the realm of the spirit. Once you have entered into the spirit realm, you can't turn back; there's nothing to turn back too. The enemy and his evil forces can hear your whining, complaints and backbiting.

Your words are moving, and they alert demonic forces of your position. Now you are open for attack. Demonic forces now want to know who you are referring too when you are speaking and they can open an attack on that person.

Let your speech be always with grace, seasoned with salt, that ye may know how ye ought to answer every man. (Colossians 4:6 King James Version)

Don't fight the Church; this is warfare! The spirits of division are real, and the slightest murmuring becomes an explosion on their territory. Have a complaint, take it to the Lord in Prayer!

Don't bring the things (flesh) of this world with you on your journey!

Soldiers assist each other in war. The enemy forces are consistent, and if the demonic forces should hear negativity in their dominions, then you're open for attack. That's why daily repentance is necessary. We all sin and fall short of the glory of Yah (God). (Romans 3:23 King James Version) You will have to repent day by day and not go back to old places of the flesh!

You are going to war for yourself, families, and the Body of Christ. Don't attack your troops verbally. Repent and move on from any hostility. You may think they are just words of general conversation, but any vile thing you say is deadly. These are the same words that hinder the Body of Christ daily and stop them from receiving from Yah (God). Sin cannot reach into the realm of the spirit and pull out blessings. The enemy and his wicked helpers are well aware of God's spiritual laws that are beneficial to the health and wealth of Yah's Children.

33 But seek ye first the kingdom of God, and his righteousness; all these things shall be added unto you. (Matthew 6:33 King James Version)

The enemy roams the earth with his evil assignments against you to hinder your blessings and destroy the livelihood of your families.

Now you can't go into his dominions with the same things (flesh, backbiting, lying, manipulating, lust, greed, etc..) of darkness he uses to attack you within the earthly realm. Children of God, you can't walk in the Power and Glory of the Lord with flesh. People of the Most High, you can't bring your contraband and wine bottle into this realm. Yah (God) needs clean empty vessels. God speaks these words, not just to you but for me also! It is a purge to clean up and prepare for a King. The things of this world are falling away and perfecting you to receive the holiness of Yah! What point would there be in the Kingdom of God if you did not change! You must repent daily and walk in the light!

7 But if we walk in the light, as he is in the light, we have fellowship one with another, and the blood of Jesus Christ his Son cleanseth us from all sin. (1 John 1:7 King James Version)

These are the exact words the Lord gave me in training fifteen years ago.

Kill the flesh! Mar 5, '04 3:19 AM

Kill the flesh!

Stomp on it!

Jump on it!

Tell it to get off of you!

Let it die!

If you want the blessing

Kick it to the curb!

Cast it into the fire!

You will survive

The flesh will not!

Flesh and deadweight

Cannot lift in

The wind of my spirit

GET RID OF IT!

I hear many speaking words of toxic people and letting go of toxic people! Are these poisonous people witches, warlocks, and sorcerers working against the Body of Christ for your demise? Or are they murmuring and backbiting sisters and brothers in Christ fighting the same demonic forces you are struggling against in life? When people are in bondage to the prince of this world, we must pray for their salvation and pray the captives are set free. We, as a people, are accountable for our sisters and brothers in Christ. Many are waking up and coming out of corrupted churches.

20 Again, When a righteous man doth turn from his righteousness, and commit iniquity, and I lay a stumbling-block before him, he shall die: because thou hast not given him warning, he shall die in his sin, and his righteousness which he hath done shall not be remembered; but his blood will I require at thine hand. (Ezekiel 3:20 King James Version)

30 Hereafter I will not talk much with you: for the prince of this world cometh and hath nothing in me. (John 14:30 King James Version)

The problem with indoctrination and traditions of men is it brings confusion, and it causes many to exit the religious Church of Christianity. How can you sit in a church, hold hands with the person sitting next to you, tell them you are going to make it, and say a prayer? Then in your next breath, tell your neighbor if you can't stand my success, then you got to go! Many say you can't take everyone to the next level with you. That's not true because I pulled people into this revelation with me, and some were not receptive, and for many, it took years even to believe. I was annoyed sometimes but not angry that I could not forgive and continue on my assignment from the Lord (Yah). I was glad when Saints of God received the revelation and understood the call. They got to the next level in the realm of the spirit to obtain from the Lord. The Lord will wait with his people.

It was those pesky demonic forces that were the hindrance with their barriers blocking the realm of the spirit, hindering my sisters and brothers in Christ (Yahusha Ha Mashiach). Remember, we are reaching into the spirit realm for our destiny, where there's resistance from the enemy. The flesh and doctrines of men want to control on this earthly platform, and Satan could care less how much you debate as long as you stay out of his dominions. Demonic forces have been strategically placed in front of you to keep you earthbound for you to contend with the dark powers of this earthly realm. They work on your mind to keep it polluted with the cares of this world to disqualify you from the race (your blessings).

STEPPING OVER MINEFIELDS

T he number one minefield Christians (believers) should avoid, is the spirit of division. This maneuver is the most devastating maneuver the enemy can plant on the battlefield of your mind. This minefield can destroy churches, families, friends, and our relationship with (Yah) God. The Body of Christ has to walk in obedience and rely on God to avoid these minefields. Choosing not to rely on Yah will bring devastation to the one who steps on the mine.

The Lord is placing his people in a position to proceed with caution.

He instructs us to step over every minefield of the enemy, which has many dangers. Saints will have to avoid all the wiles and tricks of the enemy. When satan sends thoughts of division, it is time to stand continuously with the mind of Christ and bless the one he is sending the spirit of accusation against quickly. By blessing that one, it will counteract, neutralize, and make ineffective every attempt of the enemy to infiltrate your mind and throw you off course. If the enemy can get one believer in Christ Jesus (Yahusha Ha Mashiach) to step on the mine, then turn and get you caught into his trap; that is two for the price of one. That would be considered a good day for the devil. The enemy is sending many demonic forces with the spirits of schism.

These spirits are clever little beings that wait to catch you off guard in your thoughts.

Always remember, you are warring against principalities, powers, rulers of the darkness of this world that are on your earthly realm. Once you enter into spiritual realms, you are dealing with spiritual wickedness in high places. (Ephesians 6:12 King James Version)

But he that is spiritual judgeth all things, yet he himself is judged of no man. 16 For who hath known the mind of the Lord, that he may instruct him? But we have the mind of Christ. (1 Corinthians 2:15-16 King James Version)

Now I beseech you, brethren, by the name of our Lord Jesus Christ, that ye all speak the same thing, and that there be no divisions among you; but that ye be perfectly joined together in the same mind and in the same judgment. (1 Corinthians 1:10 King James Version)

These six things doth the LORD hate: yea, seven are an abomination unto him: A proud look, a lying tongue, and hands that shed innocent blood, An heart that deviseth wicked imaginations, feet that be swift in running to mischief, A false witness that speaketh lies, and he that soweth discord among brethren. (Proverbs 6:16-19 King James Version)

10 Finally, my brethren, be strong in the Lord, and in the power of his might.

11 Put on the whole armor of God, that ye may be able to stand against the wiles of the devil.

12 For we wrestle not against flesh and blood, but against principalities, against powers, against the rulers of the darkness of this world, against spiritual wickedness in high places.

13 Wherefore take unto you the whole armor of God, that ye may be able to withstand in the evil day, and having done all, to stand.

14 Stand therefore, having your loins girt about with truth, and having on the breastplate of righteousness;

15 And your feet shod with the preparation of the gospel of peace;

16 Above all, taking the shield of faith, wherewith ye shall be able to quench all the fiery darts of the wicked.

17 And take the helmet of salvation, and the sword of the Spirit, which is the word of God:

18 Praying always with all prayer and supplication in the Spirit, and watching thereunto with all perseverance and supplication for all saints; (Ephesians 6:10-18 Kings James Version)

Wherefore gird up the loins of your mind, be sober, and hope to the end for the grace that is to be brought unto you at the revelation of Jesus Christ; (1 Peter 1:13 King James Version)

CHOSEN WARRIORS OF THE SPIRIT REALM (PROPHETIC)

Many say well, why are they chosen? They are my chosen people who fight the battles and take my people through the realms of darkness.

They walk in the spirit and will bring my people to a new level in me. Where the enemy would hinder them from receiving the fullness of my blessings, they are my front-line soldiers, who have tarried with me in the spirit. I have brought them to new heights in me. Faith to believe my word, and faith to walk by my word. They have not wavered throughout the years. They have stood on my promises not just for self but for all in my body.

In my timing, I have revealed my plan to my servants. I have given them the revelation and told them the mysteries. I am going to bless my people because I choose to says the Lord.

Those who are in rebellion will not partake. Those who follow me will inherit the land. For it is my word. It is my promise! Many are judging, but they are actually judging me, says the Lord! They are judging my ways!

My prophetic voices have delivered my people worldwide.

They have stood! My chosen vessels of honor. They run to the battle and do not seek a reward. I shall reward them, says the Lord, for their faith. I am literally going to give you lands for a possession, says the Lord.

Deeds will be written out in your names. Those that bless you I will bless them, and those that curse you I will curse them!

My people who have suffered rejection throughout the years and who are constantly being assaulted in the spirit, I say to you, depart from them around you says the Lord for their blessings are curses. They do not honor your faith or walk.

They only walk in jealousy. You desire to bless them and take them with you, and they desire to possess what I am giving you for their glory. The spirit of criticism has attached itself to you, and it is time to let it go and break that curse of attachment. Depart from me workers of iniquity says the Lord!

It will not be much longer say's God, and ye shall go forth in power and in my glory. I am removing imperfections. The people will know that the I Am is in you! What I tell you to speak, SPEAK! AND BE NOT AFRAID OF THEIR FACES!

Let the mockers mock, for it does nothing! It only reveals the heart of man and his desire to be me and write destiny the way they choose, which leads to destruction. When the church scatters, my people will run to me, says the Lord.

Those that have kept them, hostage, Woe unto the Pastors who bruise and scatter my sheep says, God!

Although they judge you now, my servants, they will honor you later. They cannot see you standing at the gate, defending my Bride. They see you make the calls of what is ahead, but they do not comprehend because they do not walk in the spirit. They choose safety instead of the battlefield.

Many of my people are not able to fight the battle I have placed you in, says God. I can only give them what they are able to bear. Make the calls says the Lord and let my people know what is ahead that they may prepare to fight the attacks of the enemy forces. Under the stronghold of fear, there are many strongholds and strongmen. The enemy is just going through a list I have already equipped you to defeat. Speak my word! Proclaim my word!

Identify the target and Destroy!

LET GO! LET GOD!

Have you ever heard the expression let go and let God? It is time to let go of this earth and reach for the things ahead for your prize. Let go of the sickness and death of this world.

Reach for the heavenly and apprehend God (Yah). Some people climb the highest mountain, sail the roughest seas. What significant challenges for man to conquer. But you are a chosen generation called to go forth and ascend from the earthly realm into the divine glory of God. The earth's problems are just too big for men to correct in their strength, power, and knowledge.

We need God's (Yah's) divine intervention that delivers, heals, and never fails. You can't go back; there's nothing to go back too! You can only press forward into the Glory of God!

The next time the devil insults you and calls you names or reminds you of someone else calling you names and how much of a failure you are, remind him that the things of this earth are just too trivial for you to overcome and you were chosen for things much too big for him and others to comprehend.

Remind him that you attend Yah's (God's) School of the Gifted. Let the devil know the first class you passed was Worship 101 in God's School of the Gifted, his old job. Then Rebuke satan!

Let's be truthful; the enemy is not just angry at you; he's in his wrath! (1 Peter 5:8 King James Version) There is a reward for being a Chosen Worshipper, which is another slap in the enemy's face. Stand in faith, knowing who you are in Christ Jesus (Yahusha Ha Mashiach)!

Take the mentality of defeat and give it back to the enemy!

Rub it in his face!

And he shewed me Joshua the high priest standing before the angel of the LORD, and Satan standing at his right hand to resist him. And the LORD said unto Satan, The LORD rebuke thee, O Satan; even the LORD that hath chosen Jerusalem rebuke thee: is not this a brand plucked out of the fire? (Zechariah 3:1-2 King James Version)

The Lord's warriors are worth a fortune! Not that the wicked want to pay you! The wicked are spending a large sum of money to stop you from coming through these realms right now. Many organizations are toiling for wealth and power in the spirit realm. Many who were assigned to bring you to your demise are not cursing you but calling you brilliant and geniuses. They want to know how you are coming through those realms: Yah's Chosen warriors, the unstoppable ones. The enemy and wicked men of the earth will always have different agendas and objectives. They will never agree in battling over your blessings! I would consider that to be a lot of confusion in the midst of darkness. The demonic forces that want access to this earthly realm will never stop insulting you or any human. Humans who play on the dark side of wickedness want wealth and control. Let me reiterate Satan hates all humanity; he wants everyone to go into the fire. That includes the witches, warlocks, sorcerers, and all those who practice wizardry, and reenactments. Let's not leave out the wicked who offer up sacrifices such as; the souls (minds) of men to demons for their lusts and greed of this world.

They practice darkness and curse the body of Christ and God (Yah) night and day. Meanwhile, Satan is plotting the demise of the wicked people on this earth. (Revelation 18 King James Version)

Greed is the cause of sickness and poverty, whether it is a human-made disease or the lack and distribution of available resources to sustain life. Satan and his evil forces have already invaded the earth. The enemy has used humankind in wickedness and made them rich throughout history to destroy God's creation. It's time for the Body of Christ to stop going through the motions of just surviving as if it's a gift from God.

1 Fret not thyself because of evildoers, neither be thou envious against the workers of iniquity. 2 For they shall soon be cut down like the grass, and wither as the green herb. 3 Trust in the Lord, and do good, so shalt thou dwell in the land, and verily thou shalt be fed. 4 Delight thyself also in the Lord: and he shall give thee the desires of thine heart. 5 Commit thy way unto the Lord; trust also in him, and he shall bring it to pass. 6 And he shall bring forth thy righteousness as the light, and thy judgment as the noonday. 7 Rest in the Lord, and wait patiently for him: fret not thyself because of him who prospereth in his way, because of the man who bringeth wicked devices to pass. 8 Cease from anger, and forsake wrath: fret not thyself in any wise to do evil. 9 For evildoers shall be cut off: but those that wait upon the Lord, they shall inherit the earth. 10 For yet a little while, and the wicked shall not be: yea, thou shalt diligently consider his place, and it shall not be. 11 But the meek shall inherit the earth; and shall delight themselves in the abundance of peace. 12 The wicked plotteth against the just, and gnasheth upon him with his teeth. 13 The Lord shall laugh at him: for he seeth that his day is coming. (Psalm 37:1-13 King James Version)

It's time for the inhabitants of the earth to fight and regain their freedom and liberty in Christ and take back the earth and heavens for all the generations to follow. Remember, the enemy can't do anything to you except invade your thoughts and cause you to war against yourself and each other to lose hope and destroy your fellow man.

1 Why do the heathen rage and the people imagine a vain thing? 2 The kings of the earth set themselves, and the rulers take counsel together, against the LORD, and against his anointed, saying, 3 Let us break their bands asunder, and cast away their cords from us. 4 He that sitteth in the heavens shall laugh: the Lord shall have them in derision. 5 Then shall he speak unto them in his wrath, and vex them in his sore displeasure. 6 Yet have I set my king upon my holy hill of Zion. (Psalms 2:1-6 King James Version)

17 "For, behold, I create new heavens and a new earth: and the former shall not be remembered, nor come into mind." (Isaiah 65:17 King James Version)

12 How art thou fallen from heaven, O Lucifer, son of the morning! how art thou cut down to the ground, which didst weaken the nations! 13 For thou hast said in thine heart, I will ascend into heaven, I will exalt my throne above the stars of God: I will sit also upon the mount of the congregation, in the sides of the north: 14 I will ascend above the heights of the clouds; I will be like the most High. 15 Yet thou shalt be brought down to hell, to the sides of the pit. (Isaiah 14:12-15 King James Version)

13 Thou hast been in Eden the garden of God; every precious stone was thy covering, the sardius, topaz, and the diamond, the beryl, the onyx, and the jasper, the sapphire, the emerald, and the carbuncle, and gold: the workmanship of thy tabrets and of thy pipes was prepared in thee in the day that thou wast created.

14 Thou art the anointed cherub that covereth; and I have set thee so: thou wast upon the holy mountain of God; thou hast walked up and down in the midst of the stones of fire.

15 Thou wast perfect in thy ways from the day that thou wast created, till iniquity was found in thee.

16 By the multitude of thy merchandise they have filled the midst of thee with violence, and thou hast sinned: therefore I will cast thee as profane out of the mountain of God: and I will destroy thee, O covering cherub, from the midst of the stones of fire.

17 Thine heart was lifted up because of thy beauty, thou hast corrupted thy wisdom by reason of thy brightness: I will cast thee to the ground, I will lay thee before kings, that they may behold thee. 18 Thou hast defiled thy sanctuaries by the multitude of thine iniquities, by the iniq-uity of thy traffick; therefore will I bring forth a fire from the midst of thee, it shall devour thee, and I will bring thee to ashes upon the earth in the sight of all them that behold thee.19 All they that know thee among the people shall be astonished at thee: thou shalt be a terror, and never shalt thou be any more. (Ezekiel 28:13-19 King James Version)

36 As it is written, for thy sake we are killed all the day long; we are accounted as sheep for the slaughter. 37 Nay, in all these things we are

more than conquerors through him that loved us. 38 For I am persuaded, that neither death, nor life, nor angels, nor principalities, nor powers, nor things present, nor things to come, 39 Nor height, nor depth, nor any other creature, shall be able to separate us from the love of God, which is in Christ Jesus our Lord. (Romans 8:36-39 King James Version)

1 The elders which are among you I exhort, who am also an elder, and a witness of the sufferings of Christ, and also a partaker of the glory that shall be revealed: 2 Feed the flock of God which is among you, taking the oversight thereof, not by constraint, but willingly; not for filthy lucre, but of a ready mind; 3 Neither as being lords over God's heritage, but being ensamples to the flock. 4 And when the chief Shepherd shall appear, ye shall receive a crown of glory that fadeth not away.

5 Likewise, ye younger, submit yourselves unto the elder. Yea, all of you be subject one to another and be clothed with humility: for God resisteth the proud, and giveth grace to the humble. 6 Humble yourselves therefore under the mighty hand of God, that he may exalt you in due time: 7 Casting all your care upon him; for he careth for you. 8 Be sober, be vigilant; because your adversary the devil, as a roaring lion, walketh about, seeking whom he may devour: 9 Whom resist stedfast in the faith, knowing that the same afflictions are accomplished in your brethren that are in the world. 10 But the God of all grace, who hath called us unto his eternal glory by Christ Jesus, after that ye have suffered a while, make you perfect, stablish, strengthen, settle you. 11 To him be glory and dominion for ever and ever. Amen. (1 Peter 5:1-11 King James Version)

BLACK BRIEFCASES ARE COMING (PROPHECY)

For the wicked have plotted and planned, and the blood of the innocent cries out to me, saith the Lord. For a price, the souls of men are sold.

Children are destroyed because of the wicked. Women are taken to the slaughterhouse of sacrifice, and the blood of the innocent cries out to me. The stench of the wicked has reached my nostrils. I said, don't turn your back on my sheep, I said deliver set free my people, the devil is trying to destroy my people. I say to the devil; I shall take thee down saith the Lord. I shall send my all-consuming fire. I shall expose the works of the wicked. I shall uncover, uncloak, unveil all of their evil. I shall require the price of the wicked, their life. They exchange money in black briefcases for the souls of men. Millions of dollars are being traded this hour. In this hour, I send my wrath upon the wicked.

Saith God!

9 And when he had opened the fifth seal, I saw under the altar the souls of them that were slain for the word of God, and for the testimony which they held: 10 And they cried with a loud voice, saying, How long, O Lord, holy and true, dost thou not judge and avenge our blood on them that dwell on the earth? 11 And white robes were given unto every one of them, and it was said unto them, that they should rest yet for a little season, until their fellow servants also and their brethren, that should be killed as they were, should be fulfilled. (Revelation 6:9- 11 King James Version)

SLEEPERS CAN BE VICTIMS OR CASUALTIES

B rethren, I count not myself to have apprehended: but this one thing I do, forgetting those things which are behind, and reaching forth unto those things which are before,

14 I press toward the mark for the prize of the high calling of God in Christ Jesus (Philippians 3:13-14 King James Version)

14 Wherefore he saith, Awake thou that sleepest, and arise from the dead, and Christ shall give thee light. 15 See then that ye walk circumspectly, not as fools, but as wise, 16 Redeeming the time because the days are evil. (Ephesians 5:14-16 King James Version)

This message for the Church is one of urgency in a sense for those in the body of Christ who are still asleep or partially awake.

37 But as the days of Noah were, so shall also the coming of the Son of man be. 38 For as in the days that were before the flood they were eating and drinking, marrying and giving in marriage, until the day that Noe entered into the ark, 39 And knew not until the flood came and took them all away, so shall also the coming of the Son of man be. (Matthew 24:37-39 King James Version)

The term asleep in this writing means that his children have not awakened to spiritual truth or have no idea what is going on in this world or with Yah (God).

9 And the great dragon was cast out, that old serpent, called the Devil, and Satan, which deceiveth the whole world: he was cast out into the earth, and his angels were cast out with him. (Revelation 12:9 King James Version)

My entire walk with the Lord, I was taught God holds you accountable for what you know, not what you don't know. I informed the same thing to others. It made sense in my mind. In truth, the Lord always made generations pay later for the sins of their ancestors.

Those whom the Israelites encountered along their journey never knew their descendants would be charged for cruelty and murder while enslaving The Most Highs people. (Genesis 15:13-16, Ephesians 6:5-9, Colossians 4:1 King James Version)

The only thing that keeps a curse going is wickedness and direct descendants controlled by satan who are fully aware of historical facts that the children of Israel were captured and kidnapped, scattered over the earth, and are continually trying to erase there existence. (Isaiah 11:12 King James Version)

However, we are blessed because we serve a merciful God through the redemptive shed blood of Christ (Yahusha Ha Mashiach) we are grafted into the vine, and we have protection from the snares (traps) of the fowler and the penalties of judgment. (Psalm 91:3, Romans 11 King James Version) We are under grace! Our God is a righteous judge.

God judgeth the righteous, and God is angry with the wicked every day. (Psalm 7:11 King James Version)

If your ancestor's identity was erased, then chances are you're a sleeper. A sleeper in this message will be referred to as a person instilled with minimal known facts or none at all of their origin. It is the awakening, and the Lord is waking up his people. Not just a rebirth for the sons and daughters of the Most High. It's a revival for the Church and every

Gentile to awake and walk in the spirit. (Galatians 5:16-18 King James Version)

The Lord God of Israel is calling his people to awaken and come out of this spiritual Babylon and not partake of her sins and plagues. (Revelation 18:4 King James Version)

Let us use this as a premise. When I first came to the Lord and was born again (saved), I don't know why I use to say this verbally, but I did, "Lord, I don't know if my great-great, great grandfather was a voodoo doctor, but I will serve you! Lord, I don't know him anyway if he goes to hell and burns he did evil." I do not know why; as a new believer, it was lodged in my mind. However, who said my ancestor was a voodoo doctor? I was associating what I have been stereotyped to believe versus what is correct. It was embedded in my mind to think that I come from evil African ancestors from a culture of Witchdoctors and inhumane people who are barbaric.

When the Lord (Yah) explained my family tree, it was a process. I began to have thoughts about my grandfather, and I was associating his appearance as a black man to my knowledge of what a Jew looked like being a white man. Yah (God) of Israel does instill impressions on your heart and in your spirit man until he's able to communicate with you entirely. The Lord made it clear that my great grandmother (Isabelle), Yah, stated, "Is mine". The Lord showed me in a vision the name Anabelle Graham Grey. The names Graham and Grey began to fade in and out like a name change had taken place. The Lord then showed me the name Benji on an old map. Then I was suddenly in someone's library of vintage books, and I could hear a man's voice say, "they must have come out of the Congo's", It was as if the man was, tracking a people. I was fully awake, listening to the Lord when he spoke and showed me the vision. I knew nothing about the Congo's or how the slave trade evolved. When I went to sleep that night, I had a dream and saw a lady and heard a voice say, snake lady. The darkness of this world came to plant darkness in my dream realm and bring it into my earth realm of belief. The voice in the dream caused me to think she was a snake lady when, in fact, she was not! The Lord spoke to me and showed me everything in the light. He could have said she was a snake lady when he showed me historical facts in the realm of the spirit in the vision.

Without a doubt, I'm convinced, the descendants of Negroes were brought on slave ships to Brazil, West Indies, and America, are the remnant of Abraham, the children of Jacob. This move of (Yah) God is not just about The Church receiving their promises and souls for the Lord's harvest but also about a commitment to gather his remnant and bring them back to their fold (group). How can I confirm Brazil? When I received the baptism of the Holy Spirit, I had a unique supernatural experience. I wrote about it in one of my writings, Spiritual Realms. The same day I received the Holy Spirit, I spoke in tongues (spiritual language) at the church altar. That night when I laid down. I was about to fall asleep; I heard a voice (God) began to speak to me, and suddenly, my room atmosphere changed, and my ceiling became stars in a night sky. Then I began to hear a massive choir sing; we are the children of Brazil, and they were thanking me for what I was doing for them in the song. I saw a white object, and I thought it was a butterfly fly down and land on my chest. I never associated it with a dove until later. I was a new believer in Christ.

And Jesus, when he was baptized, went up straightway out of the water: and, lo, the heavens were opened unto him, and he saw the Spirit of God descending like a dove, and lighting upon him: (Matthew 3:16 King James Version)

Years later, I looked up Brazil on the internet, and I read about children suffering who were orphans on the streets were being killed. I directed my prayers to pray for the children because it was children coming out of the spirit realm singing this song of gratitude.

I never associated Brazil with slavery until 2017 while streaming on the internet. Saints, I am also in the awakening. Although the Lord was using me throughout the years, he did not disclose all information to me while I've been running this race. I understood he had other runners, and they carry anointing's and assignments and purpose just as we all do in Christ.

As the sons and daughters are experiencing the awakening, more revelation knowledge is being revealed. It's like a puzzle, and all the pieces are now fitting together. It's just not a one-person show. It's to bring glory to our father in heaven. We are his willing and obedient vessels who have answered the call.

When the Lord was speaking to Abraham concerning him multiplying his seed. The Lord said, And I will gather the remnant of my flock out of all countries whither I have driven them and will bring them again to their folds, and they shall be fruitful and increase. (Jeremiah 23:3 King James Version)

17 That in blessing I will bless thee, and in multiplying I will multiply thy seed as the stars of the heaven, and as the sand which is upon the sea shore; and thy seed shall possess the gate of his enemies; 18 And in thy seed shall all the nations of the earth be blessed; because thou hast obeyed my voice. (Genesis 22:17-18 King James Version)

Let us not forget Hagar, who, according to the word, was an Egyptian slave and handmaid of Abraham and Sarah, the mother of Ishmael Abrahams's first child. Hagar received a covenant blessing also from the Lord.

10 And the angel of the Lord said unto her, I will multiply thy seed exceedingly, that it shall not be numbered for multitude. (Genesis 16:10 King James Version)

Many years ago, I had a vision, which became one of my writings, The Vision. I saw children hiding in a cave; they were different cultures and skin complexions dressed in what appeared as Indian or Arab attire. I went online to see if any clothing resembled what the children were wearing. I found a red hat; it's called a Fez. Although their hats were white, I saw a few images from people of African descent wearing something similar. A prophet told me a long time ago her interpretation; the white represented purity as if they were chosen and set apart. The male children appeared to stand out the most. No doubt, they were hidden in the cave. I interpreted them as the Sons of Glory in their birthing process. Hagar's children, the sons, and daughters of Ishmael that are about to come out of hiding. (Genesis 16:15, 21:13 King James Version)

In the vision, next to the children who were in the cave, appeared on the rock wall, an old Caucasian man with a distorted face in a transparent glass bubble shape object, and he said in a very creepy voice, "I know who you are."

The Lord God of Israel is birthing his nations of different cultures from the seed of Abraham. The only reason I still have the images in my mind because of a sister in the Lord who had recreated in detail online how I interpreted the vision. Years later, the Lord gave me a word titled The Great Unveiling (God's call to the Arab Nations). The Lord, in His Sovereignty, told Hagar her son would be a great nation; he didn't need the permission of Abraham or Sarah to deliver a promise. Our King acted on the principle of being a righteous judge towards Hagar.

According to scripture, he blessed Ishmael before Isaac was conceived. (Genesis 17:18-22 King James Version)

It is significant to know where we are coming from to know where we are going in the Lord (Yah). I don't know all the injustices that were done to the descendants of Abraham. I do know a horrific crime was committed against all the sons and daughters taken into captivity from Africa. I did hear in January 2017 the Lord singing, "We are going home."

I had a vision later that day, and I could see the most beautiful mountains and greenery, and this lady wearing what I've come to know as traditional African headwrap was leading the way. My first impression was it is beautiful, concerning the mountains and landscapes. It was like a paradise. I thought, who is this lady? I could see the headwrap and silhouette of her neck as she slightly turned her head on an angle. Perhaps an angel.

11 For thus saith the Lord God; Behold, I, even I, will both search my sheep, and seek them out. 12 As a shepherd seeketh out his flock in the day that he is among his sheep that are scattered; so will I seek out my sheep, and will deliver them out of all places where they have been scattered in the cloudy and dark day. 13 And I will bring them out from the people, and gather them from the countries, and will bring them to their own land, and feed them upon the mountains of Israel by the rivers, and in all the inhabited places of the country. 14 I will feed them in a good pasture, and upon the high mountains of Israel shall their fold be: there shall they lie in a good fold, and in a fat pasture shall they feed upon the mountains of Israel. 15 I will feed my flock, and I will cause them to lie down, saith the Lord God. 16 I will seek that which was lost, and bring again that which was driven away, and will bind up that which was broken, and will strengthen that which was sick: but I will destroy

the fat and the strong; I will feed them with judgment. (Ezekiel 34:11-16 King James Version)

I do know we can't ignore that people were stolen and sold and shipped on boats stripped of their identity and scattered all over the earth. These are biblical truths that the Lord Yah will recover the remnant of his people. (Isaiah 11:11, Jeremiah 31:10 King James Version)

I do know that I have observed in different mediums, my brown brothers and sisters mistreated in the country Israel, which could be their actual homeland.

I'm not saying that all indigenous people are the remnant seed of Abraham. However, I am implying, according to the Most High Yah, anyone who is grafted in through Yahusha Ha Mashiach is adopted into his family, which gives them full rights to live in Israel. (Ephesians 1:5, 2:8-9 King James Version)

When I read historical facts and study teachings under other doctrines, I can acknowledge where a lot of wickedness occurred throughout history. We need to thank Yah (God) for sending his son Yahusha Ha Mashiach (Jesus Christ) because the inhabitants of the earth were indeed guilty of many crimes against the people of Yah (God).

Doubt and unbelief will not be an option for the children of Yah, who want to take hold of their promises and inheritance. It's strange how some people believe in their sciences, ancestral guides, horoscopes, beasts, tea readers, religious cults, and all types of divinations but not a Creator who can do the impossible. The Lord (Yah) is calling his people to put down all their Babylonian tools and idols and come to repentance and separate yourself from the darkness of this world.

And I heard another voice from heaven, saying, Come out of her, my people, that ye be not partakers of her sins, and that ye receive not of her plagues. For her sins have reached unto heaven, and God hath remembered her iniquities. (Rev 18:4-5 King James Version)

When we partake in the enemy's devices that are designed to cause us to walk in error, we are now changing the identity of God as our Creator. Because of sin in the garden and throughout history man changed the glory of an incorruptible God to the image of corruptible man. (Romans 1:20-25 King James Version)

One reason people don't believe in a creator is that so many things are similar in the actions of those who profess to believe in God and their sinful nature. The church partakes in the same whoredoms and unrighteous acts as the world. As it is written, There is none righteous, no, not one. (Romans 3:10 King James Version)

People ask why is there sickness, evil, and death if there's a God? Believers become sick, visit doctors, and die just like an unbeliever. They don't see our faith and hear our testimonies. Many have not turned from their wicked ways, because the church has not always led as a good example. When cancer goes into remission, it is also the unbeliever's faith and testimony that science was the answer to their cure. An unbeliever does not always see God in medicine. Pharmaceutical companies that create medications to mask pain and use another medication to counteract another drug is a business, not a cure. Long term use of many medications results in organ failure and death. Turn on the television, and there are hundreds of lawsuits against pharmaceutical companies. I remember once the Lord referred to America as a sleeping giant. He said, If there were a war, we would be no use because people would choose their psychotropic medications over loyalty to their neighbor.

The Lord gave his people simple instructions to humble themselves turn from their wicked ways, then they would hear from heaven, and he would heal their land. (2 Chronicles 7:14 King James Version)

The Lord never ordained us to serve other God's or put toxins in our bodies and self-destruct. (Exodus 20:3, Jeremiah 4:1-2, Isaiah 53:5 King James Version)

Yah's word is like a verb; it takes action. Once it goes out of his mouth, it goes forth to accomplish the very thing; it is set out to reach. (Isaiah 55:11 King James Version)

The power of our tongue does the same thing; it is sharper than any two-edged sword and piercing between soul and spirit, marrow, and joint. (Hebrews 4:12 King James Version) From our mouth can come blessing and cursing (James 3:10 King James Version).

We have to learn to follow Yah's lead and instruction. Our personal experiences can't witness to everyone. A dying world needs supernatural intervention so that an atheist may believe and testify that there is a God in Heaven. Many believers in the Body of Christ have non-believer in their families and are praying for a divine intervention from God to save their loved ones. It's time for your faith to go into action and get those desired results. I fight for my family every day in prayer. I stand in the gap for them against attacks and assaults in the spirit. The enemy uses family and friends who are the closest to you many times to carry out attacks. When you become a threat to the devils already shaking, crumbling kingdom, you can expect retaliation. However, this is the season for Yah's people to wake up, repent, and armor up. It's time for them to come out of Babylon.

And they said, Believe on the Lord Jesus Christ, and thou shalt be saved, and thy house. (Acts 16:31 King James Version)

Let us look beyond our own natural ability to see with our eyes and look into the spirit with the mind of Christ. We are here today to bring the revelation on how to get him here, and that means walking in holiness, being a vessel he can inhabit for his glory. We shall be changed with a twinkling of an eye from corruptible to incorruptible. (1 Corinthians 15:53-55 King James Version)

The tree of life represents our Lord and Savior bearing twelve kinds of fruit, and we are the branches as we abide in him the vine. The leaves on the branch are for the healing of the nations. (Rev 22:1-2 King James Version)

The tree leaves represent life, that the children of God who will carry his power and glory for the healing of the nations.

Blessed are they that do his commandments, that they may have the right to the tree of life, and may enter in through the gates into the city. (Revelation 22:14 King James Version)

As we turn and render to the needs of others, the oppressed, and needy and lead them to Christ not catering to our flesh, live a life of selflessness, then our light will break out, and healing will come forth.

Your righteousness will go before you, and the Glory of the Lord will be your rear guard. (Isaiah 58:7-8 King James Version)

I am the vine, ye are the branches: He that abideth in me, and I in him, the same bringeth forth much fruit: for without me, ye can do nothing. (John 15:5 King James Version)

Whoever has ears, let them hear what the Spirit says to the churches. To the one who is victorious, I will give the right to eat from the tree of life, which is in the paradise of God. (Revelation 2:7 King James Version)

On this journey to awaken the church, let us not become bias towards other believers. If someone believes the son of God, (Yah, Yahuah) died for their sins, then they are counted as my brothers and sisters in Christ (Yahusha Ha Mashiach). The body of Christ is made up of many members, and we don't all look alike and follow the same doctrines, but we are all created in Yah's (God's) image. (Romans 12:3-6 King James Version)

The term asleep goes much more in-depth, such as missing revelation knowledge in your message. Also, to teach something you heard with no understanding is like jumping on the bandwagon or being part of a trend. Indeed, if you never heard a revelation, you can't be held accountable for not knowing. Receiving a partial revelation describes some of the truth but not in its totality. The Lord does not want his people on anymore roller coaster rides. No more thrills and excitements that only last as long as the teaching or sermon.

If the revelation is altered, it gives no precept to the listener. In other words, where's the rest of the message that takes them to a destination?

An asleep person will soon wake up suddenly and see the Church has moved into a different direction, and they have been left behind. When the bridegroom comes, you want to be prepared and have oil in your lamp and ready to enter into the Kingdom of God here on earth. (Matthew 25:1-13 King James Version) Unpreparedness is one reason the church will scatter. (Jeremiah 23:1 King James Version)

When a shepherd misses this move of God, the church members will want to know why they were not included in this vital move of God.

One reason is that many churches don't operate in a fivefold ministry such as Apostles, Prophets Evangelist, Pastors, and Teachers for the perfecting and edification of the Saint's. (Ephesians 4:11-16 King James Version) Also, many children of Yah (God) living in continuous sin, and unrepentant hearts play a crucial role within a sleeping Church. In my journey within my own family, sons and daughters have been re-indoctrinated with another gospel. This doctrine permits them to sin without conviction. Accountability is coming for teaching a false gospel, and it's a good time to repent and step down from offices Yah (God) did not ordain. (John 15:16, Ephesians 4:1, Revelations 3:15-17 King James Version)

Many whom we considered scholars, theologians, historians, and some church leaders in their own right are affirmed and awake to the truth. However, many refuse to speak the historical facts; they could care less about revelation knowledge and reality because they are too busy building their legacies instead of the Kingdom of Yah (God).

Charlatans are building a legacy on a false foundation, sending misleading messages, and exploiting millions of the Lord's people.

This revelation is not new; it has been bounced around with many leaders around 18 years, and the moneymakers made it a familiar cliché, I am Chosen. Then the wicked are in the realm of the spirit, yelling, "Chosen to do what!" Then came the stereotyping and negative comments within the church, The Frozen Chosen. Pastors also bashed "We don't need no prophets in the church," and theories on the hidden ones and whose in the wilderness and whose not. Rocks were thrown from the wicked and church leaders. Some went to their demise.

Now it's time, and the Lord (Yah) wants his spotless Bride (Church), His Harvest, and Remnant.

The world system has brainwashed us to believe a false foundation of who's who in the bible. The devil has been building his legacy before you were born. He couldn't build it in heaven, although he tried. Most infamous last quote of the enemy, I will ascend to the heavens. I will raise my throne above the stars of God. I will sit enthroned on the mount of assembly, on the utmost heights of Mount Zaphon. I will ascend above the tops of the clouds. I will make myself like the Most High. (Isaiah 14:12-15 King James Version) Strange, but I heard a female voice quoting a scripture similar to this in the realm of the spirit. Not long ago. Satan has a lot of female characteristics, which would cause me to think he is a she. That's something to ponder as new revelations are uncovered.

This plan did not work out well for the enemy (satan) when he fell from heaven like lightning. (Luke 10:18 King JamesVersion)

The enemy has brought his wrath to those that dwell on the earth and sea. (Revelation 12:12 King James Version)

Building legacies for your Glory will not last. The Lord Yahusha Ha Mashiach is our legacy. It's time for the church to arise. Wake up the young children and teens, let them know they don't need a podium with music and lights; they just need to open their mouths and worship the Lord in his beauty and holiness any time of day. (Psalm 96:9 King James Version)

The Lord has his remnant inside and outside the Church throughout the earth. He's giving them a chance to awaken from their semiconscious state of sleep. There are brothers and sisters in Christ who have left the Church evading Christianity not because they are living in sin and wickedness, but they see the deceptions within the Church.

We have been taught to believe we should stay at a place even if we're not happy. We learned by shadowing others; we come to church for God, not people. The word teaches us to fellowship and forsake not the assembly of the saints. Our leaders stress to us to be a cheerful giver, and if we're not pleasant, God doesn't want your money. Now, if you can't sing, make a joyful noise because God accepts your worship, yet in many churches, you can't be on the choir if you're not gifted to sing. Sowing seed became a roll call like an auction; five people sow a thousand dollars, fifty people sow one hundred. The worse and most hurtful is to place a timer on an offering to raise money then count to see if enough was collected.

A song of praise and thanksgiving is priceless unto the Lord. It is worth more than any tithe or offering. You vex people when you say, "If they can't give, they can't have any of the blessings that are flowing right at that particular time." That's too many inconsistencies. It's time to dissolve these indoctrinated traditions and aim at Kingdom Living with Christ. The Church needs to repent!

30 I will praise the name of God with a song and will magnify him with thanksgiving. 31 This also shall please the Lord better than an ox or bullock that hath horns and hoofs. 32 The humble shall see this, and be glad: and your heart shall live that seek God. (Psalm 69:30-32 King James Version)

We are not to be money changers in the temple of God. (Mark 11:15- 19, John 2:13-20 King James Version)

Those who run the race don't leave behind their brothers and sisters in Christ because they can't afford to sow a seed. Love (Charity) is the greatest gift.

13 Though I speak with the tongues of men and of angels and have not charity, I am become as sounding brass, or a tinkling cymbal. 2 And though I have the gift of prophecy, and understand all mysteries, and all knowledge; and though I have all faith so that I could remove mountains, and have not charity, I am nothing. 3 And though I bestow all my goods to feed the poor, and though I give my body to be burned, and have not charity, it profiteth me nothing. (1 Corinthians 13:1-3 King James Version)

Testify the good news of God's grace so that they may join the race and obtain the prize. No one has greater love than this that one should lay down his life for his friends. (John 15:13, Hebrews 12:1-3, Acts 20:22-24 King James Version)

The Lord (Yahusha Ha Mashiach) would never leave his people behind. He will give every one of his people a choice to exercise their faith and prepare for the Marriage Supper of the Lamb. (Revelation 19:6-9 King James Version)

LOVING PAST THE PREJUDICE

L ove wins souls for Christ. When saints can stop being biased and looking for human-made solutions on how to conform to the will of God, then they can win hearts.

Muslim, Jewish, Indian, whatever the culture and or religion, nothing can compare to showing love for your fellow man. Discrimination, hatred can destroy the work of a missionary and make their job harder on the spiritual battlefield, plus in the field of their everyday work!

We all know hatred is behind racism, and then behind that face lies satan. We, as believers, have to stop sending up false prayers, saying we love a culture whom we view as a threat and terror. We should not discriminate because, as believers, we were once strangers of covenant promises without Christ and no hope. (Ephesians 2:12 King James Version)

Many people stereotype all Muslims as the enemy. When in all actuality, many are fighting for their lives also. Arab brother killing Arab brother because of two different tribes is a hate crime, just like the crimes in Africa with Muslims against Christians in Sudan. We have had similar crimes throughout the US, such as gangs, Black on Black killings in the hoods of LA. Chicago and DC etc. Caucasians commit just as many crimes as any other culture, although no-one classifies them as savages or barbaric.

It's heartbreaking to see people who have one thing in common, the color of their skin to destroy each other in the name of religion. In all nations, dark or light, brown skin people still have been stereotyped and are a byword to every nation. (Deuteronomy 28:37 King James Versions) The King of Israel is delivering his people by grace, through his son Christ Jesus (Yahusha Ha Mashiach).

Yah's Chosen believes in their assignment from him by faith. Biased Christians are of no help spiritually or physically, and you don't represent Christ when you discriminate against any culture. Arab Muslims are people who want freedom and liberty, just like everyone else. They want to wake up each morning without worrying if someone put a pipe bomb under their doormat. They love their families, just like any other culture, and want to see them at the end of each day. We have to stop looking at Muslims as hateful people. We have been brainwashed to believe they are all terrible people. When in all actuality, the Arab nations were infiltrated, causing brothers to divide and separate.

Just because someone conforms to Islam and refers to themselves as a Muslim does not mean they are a pure Arab bloodline and stand for the same morals and principles. Christianity came under the guise of love when, in all actuality, it became a doctrine of devils evolving within the religion. Christ, who is the foundation, created the Church; he did not create the religion. (Matthew 16:18 King James Version) Everything planted in the Church that Yah (God) did not plant is going to be rooted up. (Matthew 15:13 King James Version)

Hate crimes still exist in America and other parts of the world today. America may not have a bomb every three days, but we have lived with burning crosses, lynching, murders, gang violence, cult violence, rapes, kidnapping, and the list goes on. Crimes against people of color (African descent) is at an all-time high. Jews murdered recently can join the ranks in schools, stores, and places of employment massacres.

Innocent children are killed in their safe places. The enemy's demonic forces could care less about children. Racism and hatred are a long slow genocide on humanity.

Who is assigning these demonic forces to come into this earthly realm and attack humanity? The enemy and wickedness is the culprit. The attacks keep people in a mourning state of their mind instead of a mode of spiritual warfare. We struggle not against flesh and blood but powers of darkness. If you want to stop senseless murdering spirits, then you have to get into the realm of the spirit and fight for loved ones through worship and prayer.

The wicked who evoke these spirits to commit crimes do it in the name of greed to obtain wealth. Next time you watch a horror or demonic film, think about what you are allowing into your spirit and mind. It's like being convinced to accept a reality that evil is a way of life. When in all actuality, you are taking this evil into your earthly sphere using books, films, and other mediums. Even if a horror happens, it should not be glorified or received as a healthy way of life. A child does not need to view any form of the mass medium where the mutilation of another human being takes place. It's time to repent and refrain from conforming to evil influences.

Many voices speak out on how barbaric another culture lives, yet our nation lives in just as much violence. Where are all our missing children and mommies in America and other countries? Who do we blame for that crime? If you can't find a rebel organization, most likely, they are somewhere training in a remote area learning survival skills. I can't blame a terrorist organization for the missing children; I don't believe they hall freight on ships and do business (witchcraft) with the souls of men (women, children, and the outcast) or care much about fancy linens and gourmet foods and spices. (Revelation 18 King James Version)

We are trying to reach a Muslim people with the love of Yahusha Ha Mashiach, and we cannot reach our people yet to stop the violence and witchcraft in our own country. We have not conquered racism in the Body of Christ, and many are talking about walking in God's Power and Glory! That would be impossible! Repent and know why you are repenting! Let the word derive be your new best friend! Everything derives from somewhere. The information superhighway online can take you to information quickly, and you can compare sources, and the truth will be evident.

Biased prayers are nothing but mere witchcraft, and it brings principalities and powers down. The next time you pray for an Arab nation, pray a prayer of love and not what God should do to Israel's and America's enemies.

Who made Arab nations America's enemy? If another country (people) is at war with Arabic nations, don't include our sons and daughters in your disagreements. America is made up of many nations, including the remnant of the Most High. The true sons and daughters of Jacob just want to go home and live in peace.

Do not be afraid to speak the truth. We have had more US Soldiers and Iraq Civilians killed since 911, since the actual count on 911 in war. We should pray that the genocide will stop in every nation!

Muslims come in all different nationalities worldwide, and many practice Islam with varying systems of belief. Jews practice their belief system in God differently also. Many are waiting on a Messiah, and many have their hand in divination. Anti-Semitism is a human-made force field that screams, you hate me because I'm a Jew. When I was young, I use to wonder why people discriminated against Jews. Since this is a crash course, to sum it up, to be an Israeli Jew today is more of a culture than an actual bloodline. How can an unbelieving Jew teach a Christian (believer) that Muslims are all bad? The ads we read are a facade, Israel and America working together to bring peace and a better tomorrow. The Body of Christ (Yahusha Ha Mashiach) is not building war allies but a Kingdom on earth for our Yah (God) in heaven to inhabit. Christians were influenced through the church according to the bible; they are supposed to provoke the Jews to repentance. (Romans 11:25-32 King James Version) Where's their repentance and salvation? How many Israeli Jews know Christ as their Savior? There are some stipulations that Christ did not fulfill the Messianic Prophecies. However, many Christians or believers walked by faith and not by sight and experienced the Father through the Son and Holy Spirit (Ruach Hakodesh) of God every day. The majority of the remnant was grafted back in through the Yahusha Ha Mashiach.

The remnant can't be the Jews that need to be provoked to repentance in the bible. It would have to be the Israeli Jews living without the Messiah as their Savior. The indoctrination goes deep when you adapt to religion and culture. Jews versus the synagogue of satan. (Revelation 3:9 King James Version)

Yah is not penalizing people who adapted to a religion or culture. He's punishing the darkness that uses them as a shield to gain spiritual power throughout the earth. Strategize someone to send an evil force or spirit shoot a temple of innocent people and collect a new fifty billion dollar budget from a country that had no participation in a Jewish Genocide. That would be the synagogue of satan at work, and the innocent people (asleep Jews) are a shield (sacrifice) along with the mentally ill person who acted out the assault.

Yet a genocide occurred here in America, transporting millions of people from Africa and putting them in bondage, and the earth has selective memory. Yah is coming with his justice, and no one can deter him from his wrath. (John 3:36, Romans 5:9, Psalm 2:12, Ephesians 5:6, Proverbs 11:4 King James Version)

Many of these Israeli (Jews) people are held hostage spiritually from the truth of their own identity. Time is almost up, and the message of salvation needs to fly over the skies of Israel. I wanted to go to Israel and live in a kibbutz, work on a farm for free and sightsee in my free time. That's the way it was explained to me if I wanted to cut expenses and travel to Israel. In my young mind, that sounded like a great deal. In my more mature mind, why would I go work for free in someone's vineyard or farm and harvest grapes for their wineries in a highly developed country? It would be insulting when you come from a culture that worked decades as brutally tortured slaves, who had awful sharecropping systems, and wage inequality throughout history.

There are a lot of impoverished countries that need free labor every day of the year. They're called missionary workers and volunteers who covet your prayers and support. People seek to honor the Yah (God) of Israel in adoration. In their mindset, helping people whom they have been taught to believe are God's chosen people is one of those ways. However, those who have the Holy Spirit of God walking in righteousness are quickened in their spirit to know the truth and then follow it by applying salve to their eyes that they may see more clearly. (Revelation 3:17-19 King James Version)

It's time for the Church to wake up and walk in their accountability to the Most High. Many will say I don't want to hear this nonsense. None the less, it's just another demonic power in the earthly realm on assignment, blinding the minds of believers to demolish the light of the glorious gospel of Christ. Walking with a spirit of superiority will close the door. Don't let the door of unbelief shut you out of the Kingdom of Yah (God) here on earth, and you forfeit your blessings. (2 Corinthians 4:4, Hebrews 3:19, Luke 13:24, John 20:29, Mathew 23:13 King James Version) Let me explain; if Yah does not get his remnant, then the church does not get their promises. Only satan and the wicked are trying to stop this move of Yah (God). The Kingdom of God suffers violence, and the violent take it by force. I'm not going to let them take it by force now that I know my opponent. Love your brothers and sisters in Christ (Yahusha) regardless of skin colors. Prejudice keeps you on the wrong team.

How can you bring peace to the earth if you hate your brother and if you don't know the Messiah, the Prince of Peace? (Isaiah 9:6 King James Version)

God of Israel says we all have to come through Yahusha Ha Mashiach (Christ), his son. (John 6:44, John 3:3, John 3:16, Revelation 3:20 King James Version) An unbeliever has more chances of hearing from (Yah) God than a rebellious house. How do I know? The Lord God of Israel is on the other side of this earthly realm waiting to collect his harvest of new souls. (Isaiah 18,19 King James Version) He knows the heart of every individual. (Psalm 44:21, Proverbs 21:2 King James Version)

Everyone wants something, The church (Body of Christ) wants their promises, True Israelites want to go home and walk into their inheritance, and God of Israel wants his new harvest of souls for his kingdom. Many people are seeking God on different roads in life. This earth has so many paths to take, and you can't judge people for searching even if it's the wrong way. In our natural human instinct, if you're thirsty or hungry, you look for water and food to quench the thirst and ease the hunger pangs. (Psalm 107 King James Version)

However, the devil has hindered the effort within many cultures to find the Lord's path. Generations of hatred that has been instilled in certain groups of people can't be dissolved overnight. Hatred derived from lies and the origin of the problem has to be eliminated to set people free throughout the earth. If someone changes their religion by choice or by force, it does not alter their bloodline. Remember, the Lord is also gathering his remaining remnant, and many are in bondage to false doctrines.

We want to pray, holy prayers up, so blessings come down on every nation. Negative words that are spoken into the atmosphere bring demons and strongholds, principalities, and dark powers down. The sons and daughters of Jacob (the remnant) need to stop complaining about the atrocity done to our ancestors, and in your same breath, you still cut your brothers in sisters down in front of a race you consider to be superior. We are not supposed to contribute to a learned behavior to help others stereotype us as people. Your demeanor is likened unto the urban term, crabs in a barrel. We, as believers in Christ, should not want to contribute any help to Satan's forces against humanity or project a regretful example of our Creator, the Most High (God). The power of the tongue does damage throughout the earth if not used according to Yah's (God's) word.

When we are led by the Spirit of Yah (God) to help a person of another culture, the Lord might lead us to tell them where their need can be met, for a good business venture, or maybe where they can get a discount on clothing. If they need food, give them the name of a good food pantry or make them a box of their favorite foods. Be kind and patient and walk in love.

Debating on religion closes doors of opportunity. We are ambassadors for Christ in the earth, and our assignment is to share the Gospel of the Yahusha Ha Mashiach, the Lord Jesus Christ. (2 Corinthians 5:19-21 King James Version)

To win souls for the Lord, plant a seed of love. Then let Yah (God) water it and take care of the rest. When we say we love people of every culture, always remember Yah is watching every action and listening to every word, thought, and intent of our hearts. (1 Corinthians 2:11-16 King James Version) Let us keep it real; some people in the Body of Christ would not even share their lavatory with a person of another nationality! It's time to Repent truly!

Racism, biased remarks, and stereotyping people of any culture cannot enter into the Kingdom of God! Prejudice It's A Spirit!

It Can't Enter The Gate!

LITERALLY, FIGURATIVELY, IRONY AND DISCERNMENT (PROPHETIC)

My words are not to be changed, switched, or placated. They lose their meaning and anointing to minister to my people. It would be like dead air. It drains the life out of my people.

My word is truth; it has a literal meaning. I do not figuratively speak and leave my people with a possibility that they cannot discern the truth. I leave them no irony that would cause them to doubt.

My word is truth, and my people that are called by name shall stand on all truth. I lead you not with feelings and emotions. I gather together my strongest in these last days to stand in the battle for my namesake. A people of no compromise. Those who compromise would cause my harvest to scatter. Those who stand in my word and truth will gather my sheep.

12 For the word of God is quick, and powerful, and sharper than any two-edged sword, piercing even to the dividing asunder of soul and spirit, and of the joints and marrow, and is a discerner of the thoughts and intents of the heart. (Hebrews 4:12 King James Version)

DOCTRINES

M any of us are not scholars or theologians, and we tend to rely on our leaders to teach and interpret the word of God for us. What we do not understand in scripture, we usually seek those who have studied for answers. (2 Timothy 2:15 King James Version) When something is broken, we find the one with the knowledge to fix the problem and give an answer or solution to the question. If my drain on my kitchen sink is clogged and leaking, I call a plumber. I don't try to pretend I'm skilled in that technique of fixing sinks or take credit for the knowledge to make the repairs.

I can't take credit for anyone's labor and accomplishments. Just like no one can take credit for your journey as you run your race. You don't have to be scholarly to come out on top in this race because you can be the plumber that fixes the sink and be first. So the last shall be first, and the first last for many are called, but few chosen (Matthew 20:16 King James Version) God said he would take the foolish things of the world to confound the wise. (1 Corinthians 1: 27 King James Version)

27 But the anointing which ye have received of him abideth in you, and ye need not that any man teach you: but as the same anointing teacheth you of all things, and is truth, and is no lie, and even as it hath taught you, ye shall abide in him. (1 John 2:27 King James Version)

People of Yah (God), this is the season of preparation for the revelation of a chosen generation. God's Chosen warriors have been running to war in the spirit for years in obedience, some with more revelation knowledge than others. I asked the Lord what he is doing because this is September 2019, and I see and hear a few parts of his revelation being revealed in different places and platforms. The Most High, our Creator, said, "I'm prepping my people." I'm not referring to false apostles or leaders and mockers who grab a piece of a revelation feed the Lord's sheep tidbits for financial gain. (2 Peter 3:3-4 King James Version) I refer to his true Shepherds (Leaders), whom the Lord can trust with revelation knowledge and carry it out in clarity.

People seek the truth, and they are known to move from doctrine to doctrine in search of all truth. Overall the Lord has revealed many revelations and mysteries too many teachers in their search for truth. Which has blessed the Body of Christ?

Be not afraid of their faces, and whatever the Lord tells you to speak, go forth and proclaim his word. (Matthew 10:26 King James Version)

Become a willing and obedient vessel, and The Most High (God) will use you for His Glory and Honor. He is using the youngest to the oldest, richest to the poorest who reciprocates his love and desires to see his will done here on earth as it is in heaven. (Jeremiah 1:8 King James Version)

I've observed the teachings of quite a few leaders in the Body of Christ throughout the years. I don't discredit their knowledge or discount them as a member of the body of Christ because of a different doctrine or culture. The Lord has blessed us with many tools for the improvement of the Church that was inspirational and encouraging. Although no man, teacher, leader prepared me for this move of God except the Most High (Yah). We don't have to agree with everyone's philosophy or culture. However, all those called by Yah are entitled to prepare for his season of readiness.

Recently, I was sitting down, and I saw a vision of an entangled vine in my mind. The closest thing I could find on the internet was some animations of tumbleweeds. I was seeing the earth intertwined with religions, doctrines, and doctrines of devils, lies, deception, greed, and the depletion of historical facts. My thoughts were, only Yah can untangle this chaos.

The Body of Christ is made up of many members for a reason. Each member supports another member in the body of Christ. Doctrines are different; however, Yah (God) is taking us to the same destination if we are willing and obedient vessels. Your intimate relationship with the Lord God of Israel is your period of growth on your journey. We will not be pointing fingers at members of the body and doctrines. The Church is made up of many cultures, and saints will have to stop hindering and intimidating people who search for truth. The Lord can and will untangle all of his people from the deceptions of the adversary. (John 20:31, Colossians 2:2-4, 2 Timothy 3:16-17, Ephesians 4:11-14, 1 Corinthians 1:21-24, 1 Peter 3:15-16, King James Version)

Many doctrines lead to the Messiah (Jesus Christ). Some doctrines have a dress code for holiness. No makeup, no heels, no dresses above the knees, and ladies must cover their hair. In some cases, if a girl became pregnant, they come before the church and repent, then marry. Women are not allowed to preach or teach under some doctrines in many cultures, and the list can vary.

Because the doctrines are different does not mean they are in bondage and don't have a relationship with Christ. In this day and age, some stricter dress codes would suffice, when we see the exploitation of our youth in today's garments. I've listened to many doctrines in the last two years of those who say they are under the law. It does not mean they don't have a relationship with him, Yahusha Ha Mashiach. Everyone must repent of their sins and accept the Messiah (Jesus Christ, Yahusha Ha Mashiach).

Many doctrines lead to Christ Jesus. We, as the sheep of his pasture, have learned to always lean towards the full Gospel of Christ Jesus (Yahusha Ha Mashiach). Many of us were taught Christianity through the church, and it's where we met our Savior. Many doctrines call our Creator by his Hebrew name or debate the spelling. Since much scripture was misinterpreted, missing, and changed, we will walk by faith and believe that (Yah) has full knowledge of all name changes. (Isaiah 65:15 King James Version) With many controversies in doctrine, it is established in the word of God that The Most High searches the heart of man. (Jeremiah 17:10, Proverbs 16:1-9, Psalms 44:20 King James Version)

Many doctrines argue the day of the sabbath, Saturday or Sunday, and the Messiah's date of birth, which causes division among many believers. Everyone is on a path for truth. Instead of being critical, seek revelation knowledge as a member of his body. Pray for one another. Allow the God of Israel to make all necessary changes on this journey to your destiny. Work as a team to seek all truth. It does not matter who was right or wrong, first or second. We should all have the same objective to meet the Lord in the air and receive his gifts to heal this earth.

When I'm walking with the Lord (Yah), I don't always want to do something, but I do it because I love him. That is what the Lord wants us to establish on this journey, unification in Christ (Yahusha Ha Mashiach), which has many members. As a family in worship, we will march right through the enemy lines in the realm of the spirit and take back everything stolen from the Body of Christ. We go as an army of believers. Worship is our warfare as we make this course correction, and Yah will personally get us back on track. The Lord wants to get a body of believers into a place where he can speak to you and guide your steps with his eye. (Psalm 32:8 King James Version) If a house is divided, it can't stand. (Matt 12:22-28 King James Version)

The enemy despises all humans, and those who believe in God of Israel are his number one target. If he can stop a body of believers from uniting as one in Yahusha Ha Mashiach, it would cause many to miss this move of Yah. The devil will pull as many as possible to hell in his final destination, the lake of fire. (Rev 12:12 King JamesVersion)

While we are under this dispensation of grace, it's time for all cultures, believers, non–believers to throw away their black magic, serpents, horoscopes, witchcraft tools, idols, charms, and whatever else you use in the occult to obtain spiritual power. Repent!

If the Lord (Yah) will close the door to his people, allow them to be scattered around the earth and let them be taken into captivity, he definitely will close it to the unrepentant wicked. (Matthew 7:22 King James Version) The Most High is no Respecter of persons. (Act 10:34 King James Version)

There are a lot of people going to heaven who renounced darkness. A great multitude are about to enter those gates to the Kingdom. Frontline warriors all know that through those gates is health, wealth, and prosperity.

What is it if a man gains the whole world and loses his own soul? (Matthew 16:26 Mark 8:34-38 King James Version)

Just like any chain of command, the ranks lowest to the highest, in darkness, works the same way. The enemy has had his followers (people) arranged as recipients operating in controlling powers and the distribution of wealth on earth for centuries, but the eternal life he was not able to master or gain. There will be no more portal openings, no keys, no back door, and no song will help the wicked get through the gate into the Kingdom of Yah (God). (John 10:1 King James Version) Mortal men who walk in wickedness want your destiny and the Kingdom of the Most High. No longer will the Body of Christ struggle to obtain their promises. The wicked stole for centuries; no longer will they get away with it in this season!

And from the days of John Baptist until now the Kingdom of heaven suffereth violence, and the violent take it by force. (Matthew 11:12 King James Version)

The next time you disagree with someone's doctrine in the Body of Christ, look at the battle you are facing as a Chosen Generation and who is your real opponent. This season the body of Christ has to put aside their differences and draw close to the heavenly Father. It's the most effective way you will be able to understand the requirements of our Creator (The Most High) as he prepares you for the Kingdom of God here on earth.

When I met the Lord and repented of my sins, it was by faith in the name of Jesus Christ that washed away my sins standing outside a prayer tent at a beach. It was an undeniable experience, and there is absolutely no way I can explain how he wrote my sins out, and I visibly saw them cross over an ocean. He guided me into his church (Full Gospel Christian Church) by way of his Holy Spirit. He used prophetic people who were precise when it came to hearing his voice and operating in his gifts. It is time for the children of Yah (God) to be accurate in their walk by eluding all circles of delusions and deception the enemy has set up for their entrapment. Do not become hung up with rituals of fasting and starving yourself to gain revelation knowledge. Faith to believe and to establish a one on one relationship with your heavenly Father will take you into his presence. No more stories that Yah (God) is moving behind the scenes with his special army. The Lord God of Israel takes you his New Glorious Church, the Bride of Christ behind the scenes.

The word of God teaches us his thoughts and ways are different from ours and much higher. (Isaiah 55:8-9 King James Version) It is time to bring clarity to the church of everything the Lord is doing through his Holy apostles and prophets. Many believers have been indoctrinated into corrupt Churches and false doctrines. Don't misunderstand; not all churches are under false beliefs, apostles, and leaders. We have very good leaders that the Lord has prepared for these end-times. There has been a powerful message for the church to repent in the last two decades. It appears there has been a revolt. An attempt to put an end to the authority of Yah (Lord). More like a mutiny in the heavens.

Many Leaders know the Lord (Yah) is calling the church to repentance, but they are superimposing the message.

The best way I can explain it is how the Lord (Yah) explained a filing system to me of the wicked. Let me backtrack because everything derives from somewhere. I found the notes from 1997 the other day. A sister in the Lord and I were visiting different churches. We felt led to visit one particular church more than the other churches in our area.

After a few visits, we felt led not to go back to the church because of the setting, and we didn't feel the presence of the Holy Spirit of God. We didn't like the atmosphere, black torch lights on each end of the pulpit, and how dark it was for a prayer service. We both agreed the chairs were comfortable, but it was not for us.

We again began to visit other churches. However, the Lord kept speaking to us both individually to go back and pray. We then returned to this church regularly. I was gullible no matter how many times this sister, who was a young prophet, told me these people are not of God. I would always say they are Christians they believe, and unless the Lord tells me differently, they are Christians. We both then began to experience bizarre things in the natural realm. My sister in the Lord was right. The church appeared like a church; it operated as a church, but the word was not being taught. When the hissing started coming from the pulpit, it was time to jump ship. We both heard and saw the same things sometimes in our natural realm. An anointed sister in the Lord, I brought her to this church, and she said there is something very wrong in this place. A few days later, she gave me a letter she typed from the Lord. The Lord was saying in the letter he equipped me for this warfare. That letter was not enough because this was too scary. The only thing that stopped us from leaving was a brother in the Lord; we knew who was a Pastor and wandered into the church while we were still visiting. We didn't alert him to any warnings; we just waited. Then strange things begin to happen to this brother in the Lord.

I had volunteered to fight principalities, powers of darkness, and spiritual wickedness in high places. I only volunteered because I couldn't see them, and I told the Lord to get someone else to deal with the people. However, I did not expect manifestations to beam into my earthly realm with the resemblance from a movie that had a character of an alien soldier to grip my heart with fear. I was young, pouring my heart out to God, telling him how I'll fight for him. I've learned in time how to take orders from the Lord and not to volunteer so quickly.

When I finally decided I'm never going back. The Lord showed me a file cabinet in a vision type of dream. In the file cabinet box, I could see cards being filed, and the Lord said, "They put the truth behind the lie, and the documents kept shuffling. The Lord said if you go back, the reward will be great! I saw Reward written out in the spirit. I immediately sat up on the bed. "I said, did you say Reward Lord, The reward will be great? I was up and dressed and out the door in less than an hour. People of God do not allow the enemy to dress up the truth with a lie to make it appear true. The Lord had a word he wanted to be delivered to that church. Some of his people were in bondage who needed freedom. Also, the Lord just wanted me to go back in obedience and show no fear. Do not be afraid of them, for I am with you and will rescue you," declares the Lord. (Jeremiah 1:8 King James Version)

Pray for an anointing of the Holy Spirit to fill your temple and lead you into all truth. People of God, you will need an anointing from God and the gift of discernment to break free from these deceptions. A corruptible new-age church has influenced many children of God. Sons and daughters of God, prepare your temple to become a glorious church without spot or blemish for the Most High to inhabit. (Ephesians 5:27, 1 Corinthians 6:19 King James Version)

The Lord loves you and desires for you to come into his presence. Your relationship with the Father is pertinent to your destiny. Every decision you make after reading this message is relevant to your future. Worship is your warfare! No Church choir is required to worship and come into the presence of the Most High God. (1 Corinthians 6:19, Matthew 18:3 King James Version)

I'm always learning with my reservations; however, I walk in freedom and liberty in Christ to examine the doctrines and try every spirit. (1 John 4 King James Version) Remember, do not be deceived; you will not be able to ride on the labor of anyone's anointing to enter into the Kingdom of Yah (God) here on earth. Repent daily talk to the God of Israel, your Creator, and establish your love story.

THE BATTLEFIELD 101

The Lord's battlefield, it is made up of male, female, young, old, the remnant, forerunners, and frontline warriors from all nations.

They are all grafted into the branch through the son of Yah (God). Overall this is a Chosen generation. The Sons of Glory will be birthed, and the few Chosen are all women. It's not a feminist movement but a strategic move by Yah. He has chosen a few means Chosen for spiritual warfare. A move the enemy never saw coming. God is no respecter of persons. (Romans 2:11 King James Version) He is going to bless his people worldwide. Just a few simple instructions and obedience will bring you out of the darkness of this world into the light of the Living God.

Righteousness is the key to coming through this realm. You have to acknowledge your thoughts and the way you think, and your flesh has to die. You can't pretend your way through this move of God. It will not work because you have to come through a spiritual realm. Demonic forces will not let you pass in your flesh. They will detain you, make a plan to deter (discourage, instill fear), then throw you off course.

7 For as he thinketh in his heart, so is he: Eat and drink, saith he to thee; but his heart is not with thee. (Proverbs 23:7 King James Version)

The Lord is calling every one of his children to a daily repentance. We are to draw closer to the Father through our repentance of daily sins. He loves you unconditionally through all your mistakes in life. He's always calling your name to return to his love. What's so beautiful is we never get too old to be cuddled by God. He's ancient, so no matter how old you get on this earth, you're still a child of the King. When things are not going right in your life, he is always there, ready to dry your tears and give wisdom for your problems. Never think your sin is so big you can't return to his love. Christ died on the cross (tree) so that you could be in the presence of our Heavenly Father. We all have sinned and fall short of the Glory of God, and we are justified by grace. (Romans 3:22-24 King James Version) There is no condemnation for them that are in Christ. (Romans 8:1 King James Version)

I began receiving Proclamations and Revelations in 1994. It was as if the Lord just started downloading from his Spirit to my Spirit. There was nothing perfect about me or my life. I hope these writings and messages from the Lord assist you on your journey as you prepare to enter into the Kingdom of God here on earth. I pray you obtain your inheritance as the sons and daughters of Yah. The Lord gave me this message about the future of his people. I'm referring to the destiny of a chosen generation who are about to walk into the supernatural and do greater works than Jesus Christ (Yahusha Ha Mashiach). (John 14:12 King James Version) I also speak of the remnant who will be returning home and the new harvest of souls entering the kingdom.

I speak to the warriors and frontline soldiers of all cultures.

You have fought for years in the realm of the spirit and followed orders from the Lord in compliance and did not break ranks. Many of you had no title or platform, and you ran to battle in obedience. You will do the greater works. (Joel 2:7 King James Version)

They are fighting for the Church out of obedience and a willingness to take orders from the Lord. Children of Yah, this is your season to go forth in the Spirit of the God of Israel and run your race. (Hebrews 12:1-3 King James Version)

The Lord has prepared preachers, teachers, prophets, apostles, and evangelists that will not compromise and are ready to assist him with his new harvest. Some warriors, because of the intensity of warfare, moved on to be with the Lord. Always remember in war, there will always be casualties, and some victims caught in the crossfire. The same principle applies to spiritual warfare. For the children of Yah (God) to be absent from the body is to be present with the Lord. (2 Corinthians 5:8 King James Version)

Imagine your mind as the battlefield. Example: your neighbor keeps coming over complaining, telling you all his problems and complaints. You try to help with each encounter. Then you realize the stories are not matching; they keep changing. Then suddenly, you realize they are lies. That's exactly how the enemy operates on the battlefield of your mind. You want to go somewhere that will help you in life, but your thoughts keep changing and deterring you from moving on to a new designated place.

It's all about your mind and how you respond to the truth or a lie. The devil is very subtle; he's a manipulator. The enemy can't do anything except tempt you to believe a lie. If you can get past his lying spirits, then you are moving in the realm of the Spirit.

We wrestle not against flesh and blood but principalities, against powers, against the rulers of darkness of this world, against spiritual wickedness in high places. (Ephesians 6:12 King James Version)

The Lord wishes all his seasoned warriors who became wearied get back in the race and allow him to bind up those wounds. (Psalm 147:1- 5 King James Version)

The Church can't go back and change their past mistakes, but we can strive now as the Body of Christ for the promises of God and walk in his righteousness. We are uniting as one body in our Messiah (Christ). And if a kingdom be divided against itself, that kingdom cannot stand. (Mark 3:24 King James Version)

Some sons and daughters will have to leave the Spirit of religion and doctrines behind. The Lord will instruct you what you must surrender to take his assignment. The Spirit of religion will hinder you at every turn to deter you from walking in your Freedom and Liberty in Christ. Spirits are assigned to this earthly sphere to take up residency and rule over your mind. They want full control. A Principality is a spiritual prince that wants a place to reign. Your governments, churches, corporations, wherever there's a place for rulership, these demonic forces will try and infiltrate and set up their dominion in this earthly realm.

We are in a world which is dying from the onslaught of the enemy. The Church can't put a bandaid on sickness any longer because the church has become ill with sin. The Lord's people need the power to fight these vicious attacks from the enemy and his evil forces. For many years the Lord has been preparing his army of Prophets. He's coming for his Bride (The Church) without spot or blemish. His sons and daughters who have chosen to walk in righteousness. (Matthew 6:33 King James Version) If Yah can prepare an army of prophets to walk in righteousness and holiness, and they can come through a realm, so can the Church. Many do not walk with the title of Prophet or Apostle on their name; however, it does not mean they have not answered the call. It's not the title, but focusing on accomplishing their assignments from Yah (God).

There is still time to get ready. There is no specific gender or age the Lord is calling. He will use the youngest to the oldest and the richest to the poorest. Holiness and righteousness is your requirement. All those that love him are invited into Yah's Kingdom. The Lord just spoke these words to my Spirit, "For such a time as this "! It's a phrase that comes from the Book of Esther 4:14 King James Version.

You might wonder what it means for you as a son or daughter of God? It means walking in the full manifestation of the God of Israel here on earth in the demonstration of his Power and Glory. There have been delays throughout the years; however, it is not because of the sheep. It is because we fight a real adversary. The good news is that the Lord has prepared a path for you, his Church. There are going to be many who say I don't want to take the path of the church. I hope that in obedience and establishing a genuine relationship with Yah (The Lord), you will see that he's replacing a corrupted church with a Glorious Church. True healing comes when we forgive and allow the Lord to go to work in our hearts, and we walk in love and humility. We forgive those that trespass (commit an offense) against us. A true Israelite can't hold a grudge against a member of their family; it would be like holding a grudge against Yah (God). When Yah asks, he is so kind there's no way you can say no to him. If you say no, he'll keep asking over and over again. Occasionally he will turn up the volume and leave you with no doubt he is speaking. He sometimes explains his reasons why he wants something done. Then if you're not budging, he'll often let you feel the urgency. Those are my personal experiences and a few other sisters and brothers I know who were called to the battlefield. Your experience might be similar or different. It's your own experience with our Creator that makes you a believer. Our Lord God of Israel came and rescued you and delivered you in your time of need. He heard your cry and request, and he answered through his son. (1 Kings 19:12 King James Version)

If you love him, you will accept his invitation to be transformed into his image from corruptible to incorruptible.

51 Behold, I shew you a mystery; We shall not all sleep, but we shall all be changed, 52 In a moment, in the twinkling of an eye, at the last trump: for the trumpet shall sound, and the dead shall be raised incorruptible, and we shall be changed. 53 For this, corruptible must put on incorruption, and this mortal must put on immortality. 54 So when this corruptible shall have put on incorruption, and this mortal shall have put on immortality, then shall be brought to pass the saying that is written, Death is swallowed up in victory. (1 Corinthians 15:51-54 King James Version)

The voice of one crying in the wilderness, Prepare ye the way of the Lord, make his paths straight. (Mark 1:3 King James Version)

The Lord is gracious and kind, and he wishes that none should perish. Church, this is your assignment from The Most High. Join the race and run. (1 Corinthians 9:24-27 King James Version)

Christianity, throughout history, has derived from much darkness. The Lord (Yah) has taken many routes to bring his children into the light and promises of this day. The enemy had many plans to destroy the church, the remnant, and the harvest because he knows his time is short. However, this season, you will become equipped as the body of Christ ready to proclaim the good news and defeat the enemy at every turn. The Lord gave simple instructions as you run your race. Do not fight the Church!

This revelation is for believers in Christ (Yahusha) who want to win and walk into their promises and inheritance. Not everyone will agree with this revelation. We have been persuaded to believe scholars and theologians directed us to all truth. When, in fact, the Most High has to reveal the truth to his people. The word states God does nothing unless he reveals his secrets to his servants, the prophets. (Amos 3:7, 1 Corinthians 2:9-12, Ephesians 1:17 King James Version)

The Gospel of Jesus Christ (Yahusha Ha Mashiach) is all truth. He died for the sins of the world. If it were not for the Lord's church and those who had faith to stand generation after generation, we would not be in this revelation. (Matthew 16:18, Colossians 1:18, King James Version)

I tell those who are trying to take this revelation and run a different way for their Glory; it will not work. It will only bring division to your churches and camps. I see the Lord has chosen very young sons who walk in obedience from an Israelite camp that will be transformed as his Sons of Glory and demonstrate his power. He has not dismissed his people. As his people search for truth, he will meet them at every turn.

This word might sound repetitive in this writing; however, it's imperative that regardless of what you see or hear in the church that's not of Yah (God), stay in prayer for the Saints (children) of God and his Remnant. Don't lose integrity or allow anyone to take you out of character and cause you to sin. It's not easy, but it's doable. Walk-in righteousness and use edifying words. Speak the truth as the Lord reveals. It will save a life.

10 See, today I appoint you over nations and kingdoms to uproot and tear down, to destroy and overthrow, to build and to plant."(Jeremiah 1:10 King James Version)

From my own experience, it is very easy to deviate. The closer you get to the King, the more the enemy will bring flesh to provoke you to sin. I sat under a Pastor who used to say; God does not care how many times you fall; he just wants to know which way you are standing when you get back up. Holding our tongue is a battlefield because words can heal or do a lot of damage. (Psalms 64:4, Luke 6:45, Proverbs 21:23 King James Version)

We are not perfect. The best warriors fight the same battles as every other believer struggling to win on the battlefield of the mind. The worst action is camp invasion through family and friends. The enemy uses the people we love at times as vehicles of assault because these are the people who are the closest to our hearts. We will have to combat the Spirit of division (Jezebel) always until we meet the Lord in the air. (1 Kings 18:4, 1 Kings 19:1 King James Version) The darkness covering the earth is not a metaphor. (Isaiah 60:2 King James Version) Start your journey with the Lord and move out of the darkness of this world. The Lord has Prophets who are equipped to deliver his messages and corrections to his leaders. You do not have to engage in arguments with the body of Christ. This invitation is open to all leaders. They also are starting a new journey out of the darkness of this age. We are breaking old traditional habits and stepping out into revelation knowledge. Always remember, don't fight the church; we were all sinners and we are forgiven by grace by our Creator through the shed blood of Christ, his son (Yahusha Ha Mashiach). There is no time for the sheep to turn back and judge because you have your assignment now from the Lord. (Romans 3:23-26 King James Version)

It should be made clear that we are moving from the corruptible Church to the incorruptible Kingdom.

If anyone says we are in the kingdom of God, then ask them why his people are still divided, cussing, drinking, lying, manipulating, and stealing, walking in envy, and strife. We have not yet arrived! The kingdom is within you, the flesh has to die, and then we will be activated an unstoppable Bride. We are not bringing the kingdom to a corrupted church; we are taking a church without spot or blemish to the Kingdom of God, which is incorruptible. This transformation is going to be supernatural. It only takes faith to believe and to follow the Lord's lead. Acknowledge that he is right here with you waiting for your yes to his invitation, the Marriage Supper of The Lamb. (Revelation 19:6-9 King James Version)

The Lord (Yah) chose me before I was conceived in my mother's womb. (Psalm 139:13 King James Version)

I am the remnant of Yah behind the scenes with the Lord. I am his bloodline chosen to assist and bring his church into his presence. My genealogy goes back to my great-grandmother. The Lord (Yah) said she was mine"! Without a doubt, I know who I am in the Lord. I will attest to the fact you are a chosen generation from all nations bought with a price the blood of Jesus Christ (Yahusha Ha Mashiach). There should be no division between the church and his remnant on this journey. We are both grafted in through Yahusha Ha Mashiach (Christ Jesus).

The God of Israel will bring you his true remnant who were scattered over the earth to their birthright. Our Father in heaven is a righteous judge.

There have been many oppositions, accusations, assumptions, and racism throughout the years of saint's striving against one another for the title of Chosen. It was never about a platform; it was all about the Shepherd, King of Israel, and the sheep of his pasture, which have a promise. A Chosen generation called by God to come out of the darkness into his light. (Psalm 95:7, 1 Peter 2:9 King James Version)

HISTORY 101

T hat we henceforth be no more children, tossed to and fro, and carried about with every wind of doctrine, by the sleight of men, and cunning craftiness, whereby they lie in wait to deceive; (Ephesians 4:14 King James Version)

Many servants of the Lord have left the church and moved out from under the guise of Christianity. Some have started camps and declare they abide by the law. Many have become lost in the law and doctrines and don't agree on anything as a tribe. Some have fallen into habitual sin and don't even follow the law. (Romans 2:1-16 King James Version)

The Most High is calling his sons and daughters to change a few things by allowing him to work out all the offenses and injustices committed against them as a people to heal their scars. (Deuteronomy 32:35 King James Version) The Lord wants you to be at peace with all men and walk into your inheritance. This inheritance is your portion from Yah (God) as a believer who walks in obedience and holiness, accomplishing his will on earth. (Ephesians 4:29 King James Version)

He's calling his sons from the tribe Judah to walk as His sons of Glory. Yahuah (God) is going to deliver you, not a human-made government. The next time a brown skin man puts a chain around his neck and calls it jewelry and fashion, think about black men in neck chains and shackles, taught to believe in bondage unconsciously. The enemy has lost this fight, children of Yah.

Dearly beloved, avenge not yourselves, but rather give place unto wrath: for it is written, Vengeance is mine; I will repay, saith the Lord. (Romans 12:19 King James Version)

The revelation might go against your beliefs, traditions, and doctrines, but the Father has awakened us to walk into our inheritance. Everyone must repent and go through the son Yahusha Ha Mashiach (Lord Jesus Christ) to enter into the Kingdom of God. The Lord is going to do his divine intervention into the hearts of his people. It's Yah's Kingdom, and we all have to re-adjust to the way we perceive and believe in how the Most High will move on behalf of his people.

8 For my thoughts are not your thoughts, neither are your ways my ways, saith the Lord.

9 For as the heavens are higher than the earth, so are my ways higher than your ways and my thoughts than your thoughts. (Isaiah 55:8-9 King James Version)

We have had very good scholars and theologians throughout history who search out historical facts and truth. And they are true to their profession and calling. However, theologians and scholars wrote multitudes of books on the end-times, and rapture made a lot of money on false doctrine and teachings. Some knew the truth, and for many, it was a pattern taught from generation to generation. Now it's time for all believers to stop teaching false doctrines, whether you knew it or not and repent. It's time to seek the Lord, Yah of Israel, in prayer for all truth in his word. It is your faith, love for Yah, and personal relationship that will bring you to your final destination. Whatever doctrine people are practicing, it's time to drop the principles of men and prepare to enter into the Kingdom of God. Saints of God, you can't get into the Kingdom serving a carnal nature. You might have heard throughout the years the church is teaching replacement theology to replace the Jews throughout the years. We're not replacement theology. Those very words contribute to building a wall of defense around people who are still asleep. The synagogue of satan masterminds these deceptions to cover their illusions. The Lord is delivering a covenant promise to the Church, his Bride, and his true remnant. Let us not forget he's coming to rescue his new harvest of souls. We all have the same adversary, and if it were possible, he would lull us all back to sleep.

9 Behold, I will make them of the synagogue of Satan, which say they are Jews, and are not, but do lie; behold, I will make them to come and worship before thy feet, and to know that I have loved thee. (Revelation 3:9 King James Version)

14 And the Lord God said unto the serpent, Because thou hast done this, thou art cursed above all cattle, and above every beast of the field; upon thy belly shalt thou go, and dust shalt thou eat all the days of thy life: 15 And I will put enmity between thee and the woman, and between thy seed and her seed; it shall bruise thy head, and thou shalt bruise his heel. (Genesis 3:14-18 King James Version)

This battle started in the garden because of disobedience to Yah! Now it's the season of deliverance for a chosen generation. His people will walk into their inheritance as the sons and daughters of Yah (God). The remaining remnant and gentiles are adopted by grace and grafted into his branch by his son (Yahusha), our Savior. (Romans 11:11-24 King James Version)

There are no shortcuts to the Father or his kingdom. We all have to be grafted in by the redemptive blood of Yahusha Ha Mashiach (Christ) to receive the promise. (Ezekiel 36:19-24 King James Version)

If we must receive Yahusha Ha Mashiach (Jesus Christ) by faith, then it's the season for the Jews to repent and begin their faith walk and healing process. How long does it take to ask (Yahusha Ha Mashiach) to forgive you for your sins and repent? It's free! Do not allow the enemy to hinder you from all truth. There is only one way to the Father, and that's through the Son (Yahusha Ha Mashiach). It is by faith we receive the son of Yah. I want there to be some clarity and understanding of who's who in this crash course. We have to know where we are coming from to know where we are going.

Many Jews are indoctrinated to believe they are the original bloodline of Yahusha Ha Mashiach because they can carry the title of Jew; however, it just does not qualify them as a chosen people unless they are grafted in through Yahusha Ha Mashiach (Christ Jesus). There are many Jews throughout the world who have received Christ as their Lord and Savior. They understand the principle of being grafted into the vine (God), yet they are asleep about their origin. A lot of truth is lost in history and erased. We can't disqualify all Jews from this race or invitation from Yah. Some found truth and accepted Yahusha as their Lord and Savior. The traditions and teachings of men influence the Jews who have not accepted Yahusha Ha Mashiach. You can't penalize people who were taught to believe they are a chosen people through a bloodline if they are not knowledgeable. The synagogue of satan that points to a darker side of greed, notoriety comes under the disguise of a Jew. The darker side that keeps Israeli Jews in bondage to a false doctrine of their identity.

29 Woe unto you, scribes and Pharisees, hypocrites! because ye build the tombs of the prophets, and garnish the sepulchers of the righteous, 30 And say, If we had been in the days of our fathers, we would not have been partakers with them in the blood of the prophets. 31 Wherefore ye be witnesses unto yourselves, that ye are the children of them which killed the prophets. 32 Fill ye up then the measure of your fathers. 33 Ye serpents, ye generation of vipers, how can ye escape the damnation of hell? (Matthew 23:29-33 King James Version)

Yahuah is the Creator, and he is no respecter of person. He has the same love for the Jew as he has for the remnant and gentiles. We know that the remnant is not a large number of people and that the promise to Abraham would be through adoption, grafting people in through the redemption of sins by the shed blood of Yahusha Ha Mashiach. The mistake mere men continue to make is to commit genocide against people of color. Assignments issued under the direction of satan and wicked leaders through sterilization, abortion, and cold-blooded murder through population control.

The sons and daughters of Yah (The Most High) must walk by the Spirit and in Truth and not accept any part of the world's system of darkness to destroy human life. (Galatians 5:16, John 16:13, Matthew 23 King James Version)

Yah (God) is not the author of confusion but of peace as in all churches of the Saints. (1 Corinthians 14:33 King James Version) The time of the

Gentiles has come, and the Lord has grafted his people into his branch. He has grafted back in the seed of Abraham his True Israelites (Chosen people, his bloodline). Jews (Israelis) who believe in the son of Yah (God) are also grafted into the branch. (Romans 11:11-31 King James Version) Those who are not grafted in through the shed blood of Yahusha Ha Mashiach for the redemption of sins are under a false doctrine. Ashkenaz of European descent, who through their ancestry converted to Judaism, has the opportunity to repent and receive Yahusha Ha Mashiach as their Savior! The door is open for anyone who says they are Jews and want to receive Yahusha Ha Mashiach (Christ) as their Lord and Savior.

"No more pointing fingers at the Palestinians, as if they stole something from you, says Yah." The door is open for all of humanity to repent. (Genesis 10:1-5, 1 Chronicles 1:6, Jeremiah 51:27) (2 Peter 3:9 King James Version)

THE BATTLEFIELD 102

R emember, the church will not be able to get away with what they got away with in the past. You cannot bring the things of the world with you on your journey with your new relationship with your Father in heaven. There will be no portals open to the wicked or false apostles to operate through to stop you from reaching your destiny. They will no longer be in your way on your path to the Father (The Most High). That means you will have no hindrances if you repent daily, worship each day, which will be your warfare. Remember to cast down those big imaginations that exalt themselves against the knowledge of Yah (God).

If you follow the Lord's lead, Satan's forces can't hinder your journey. The Lord (Yah) is going to empower those in the church who love and seek him in this season. The church has been suffering for decades. People will come to Christ (Yahusha Ha Mashiach) to be delivered and set free worldwide from the Power and Glory that the Lord will place upon those who can believe by faith to enter into his gate in holiness. The Lord said he wants his church, his Bride. Which means he's going to change the condition of his church to bless his people.

The Body of Christ has many members worldwide who love the Lord but can't afford to feed themselves or their families. It's your season for their deliverance. It is spiritual bondage to live in a world that has so many resources, and the people do not prosper and go hungry.

Years ago, I was running in the realm of the Spirit, and I saw a gate with tall iron bars. On the other side of it were people as far as I could see who appeared to be of Asian descent. There was a thick fog, and there were so many people I could not see the end of them. I heard a voice say these people don't go to heaven. The realm was so massive in deception; you believed the deception when you came out of that realm of the Spirit. All praises to God the domain no longer has a gate, and those souls are free. The captives will all go free. The word of the Lord is that none should perish. How can you choose if you are locked up behind bars spiritually with no freedom to make a decision? It's not much of a choice if you do not know you are in spiritual bondage.

I had a dream not very long ago, and a woman of Asian descent spoke from across a room. Then she said use foo to buy more foo. At first, I could not understand her dialect. I know she was saying for me to buy something, then I saw items on the grocery belt at the cash register. Finally, I realized it was her broken English. She was giving the warning to buy food stock up. She meant to use food to buy more food. On the belt in the basket with groceries, a brown bottle stood out that resembled an old fashion medicine bottle. I assumed you buy not only food but also purchase medication, which would be like a type of bartering system as if money had no value. She was translating the warning into English.

It leads me to believe a food shortage is coming. This dream reminded me of my very first writings on spiritual realms, where I had a vision the grocery store shelves were almost empty and in another country was some type of chemical warfare happening, and people were struggling to breathe. I wrote a pamphlet called Josephs Table and posted an emergency list online years ago to use in stocking pantries and emergency items. We never know how Yah (God) will use his people from all over the world in these end-times to deliver messages, warnings, and confirmations. People of Yah (God) stocking a pantry and learning to rotate groceries, canning, or growing vegetation should be a sensible approach to not trust the world's system to deliver your necessities in an emergency where there's chaos. In this season, the people of Yah (God) should always keep a pantry for emergencies. The times are too unpredictable to rely on stores to stay stocked when most stores operate on supply and demand. If some of you have not noticed, many fruits and vegetables are seedless. They cannot be reproduced. If you can't harvest seeds from your produce (farming or garden), you are relying on someone else for your food supply. We should all stock up for at least a year of food and water and stay on rotation. There are many videos on the internet to assist you in keeping a bug and rodent free pantry, or closet. We have had terrible storms, and the government was not prepared or equipped to help a large mass of people in chaos. It was the church and neighboring states with people of compassion that open their doors and homes for the desolate.

Your blessings are in the spirit realm, and the wicked enjoy feasting off of your blessings. They don't just hang in the domains to put you behind spiritual bars and curse you. They like stealing from you.

There's no way to know they are stealing. It's not like someone taught every believer or unbeliever on earth how to combat this type of warfare. The thief comes to rob, kill, and destroy is the most we learned in an average church service. If the devil is robbing people, he must have somewhere to put the goods. The hands of the wicked to continue his kingdom on earth. He needs his vessels to do evil, just like Yah (God) needs us as vessels to do good. (John 10:10 King James Version)

Worship is your warfare! If you can learn to worship and give Yah praise on an ongoing basis daily, you are going to be more effective in combat. Turn on the radio, listen to worship music, lay prostrate before the Lord, and or cry out to the Lord. However, you worship, allow the Holy Spirit to lead you. Some of you may say I already worship the Lord daily. However, this time you will be on an assignment as the Bride of Christ, a vessel without spot or blemish!

Worship will be your warfare. The power of your voice will move demonic forces out your way in the realm of the spirit. In your place of worship, whether it be your prayer closet, car, kitchen, church, as long as you worship, you will begin the process of moving closer to the Lord. Run your race! Others will be running with you in the Spirit.

Worship! Worship! Worship!

If you have a beautiful place to fellowship with believers and it has blessed you and others in need, support the house of the Lord (Yah). The Lord loves a cheerful giver does not mean give away all your money and not have finances to meet your daily needs. Do not suffer in your giving, (2 Corinthians 9:6-7 King James Version) The poor support the church when it should be the church supporting the poor. (Deuteronomy 15:11, 24:14, Psalm 12:5, 14:6, 34:6 King James Version)

The Lord loves a cheerful giver, and if you not cheerful, then keep your money, which is another indoctrinated tradition. If you are living paycheck to paycheck just making ends meet or below poverty, keep your money in your pocket. The Lord would not even take your money. Do not be deceived. Sow seeds a different way and share the gospel of Christ and how he saved your life. Yah's people are just tired of going around in circles in churches and coming out in the same condition as they walked into the church. We attest to the forgiveness of sins through Christ as a real experience, and now we want the promises for that faith to believe.

They tell you that you should not be in the same condition when you leave. That's another indoctrination of tradition. That's why many have left the church. The situation was not changing, and they were thirsty for God and going broke in their giving. (John 4:14,7:38, Revelation 21:6 King James Version)

WORSHIP IS YOUR WARFARE

Y ou are probably wondering what happens when we follow these steps. It will be a gathering of the saints. Except it will not be a rapture, which is not in the bible. Caught up is written in the scriptures. Then we which are alive and remain shall be caught up together with them in the clouds, to meet the Lord in the air: and so shall we ever be with the Lord. (1 Thessalonians 4:17 King James Version)

The dead in Christ are to rise up first. If you're wondering why the dead go up first, it's because they never actually crossed over yet to heaven to be with the Father (Yah).

We are taught to believe they crossed over, but they are with Christ (Yahusha Ha Mashiach). I always wondered why do people say, Rest in peace, if our loved ones crossed over to heaven. The Lord Yahusha Ha Mashiach told the thief who was hanging, today you will be with me in paradise. (Luke 23:40-43 King James Version)

Just like Abraham carried the children of God in his bosom until Christ died and was resurrected. Christ carries the dead. (Luke 16:19-31, Isaiah 40:11 King James Version) When the Bride of Christ (Church) moves through this realm, then we will be caught up simultaneously to meet the Lord (Yah) in the air.

39 And knew not until the flood came and took them all away, so shall also the coming of the Son of man be. 40 Then shall two be in the field; the one shall be taken, and the other left. 41 Two women shall be grinding at the mill; the one shall be taken, and the other left. 42 Watch therefore: for ye know not what hour your Lord doth come. (Matthew 24:39-42 King James Version)

I'm sure you heard this word preached concerning the rapture. If it had come by revelation knowledge, it would be great, but the assumption does not take the Church to destiny. Tradition will stick with the old philosophy that God will lift you off the earth in the tribulation as your protection.

After decades of preaching to sheep (people) a rapture theory, it's time to stop the charade of selling books and CDs to save face. I'm not including leaders who are asleep. The leaders that are awake and know the truth will be judged by Yah (God). Many with platforms were told the revelation, and instead of retracting the false information, they choose to keep the saints in bondage with half-truths. They don't want to say you're going up in the air in this season, and the Lord is going to deliver you a package with Power and Glory. The reason is that you won't need to rely on the one-person-show in the pulpit any longer, and you won't be thirsty for a word. Yah is not going to meet us in the air and leave people to perish here on the earth. Those people left behind would be friends, relatives, and his new harvest of souls for his Kingdom. He wants his harvest more than false replicas of leaders on platforms who would leave a people in the hands of a destroyer. We are the chosen generation and we are coming out of the darkness into his light. Which means we are waking up to all truth. We were all under the shade of deception. The Lord is giving his people time to repent, which means to stop intentionally selling a lie for wealth and fame. This season we should fear Yah (God) and repent. There's not much of a choice when it comes to missing (raptured) on earth, and Yah (God) throws you in the lake of fire alive. If you're alive, it does not sound like the second death but the first. (Revelation 19:20 King James Version)

Our Lord and Savior will be traveling with us when Yah (God) pulls us through into his Glory and Power. The most significant moment in history is when the son Yahusha Ha Mashiach shall be Glorified with the Father (Yahuah) in heaven. Then the Bridegroom turns around and starts coming back into the realm of the earth leading his army of chosen warriors, the Bride of Christ and his Holy Angels, carrying all Power and Glory to destroy wickedness upon the earth.

62 And Jesus said, I am: and ye shall see the Son of man sitting on the right hand of power, and coming in the clouds of heaven. (Mark 14:62 King James Version) 26 And then shall they see the Son of man coming in the clouds with great power and glory. (Mark 13:26 King James Version) Your enemies will not see death until the King of Kings comes in his glory. Yah (God) is Coming!

5 Thou preparest a table before me in the presence of mine enemies: thou anointest my head with oil; my cup runneth over. 6 Surely goodness and mercy shall follow me all the days of my life: and I will dwell in the house of the Lord forever. (Psalm 23:5-6)

27 For the Son of man shall come in the glory of his Father with his angels, and then he shall reward every man according to his works. 28 Verily I say unto you, There be some standing here, which shall not taste of death, till they see the Son of man coming in his Kingdom. (Matthew 16:27-28 King James Version)

13 I saw in the night visions, and, behold, one like the Son of man came with the clouds of heaven and came to the Ancient of days, and they brought him near before him.14 And there was given him dominion, and glory, and a kingdom, that all people, nations, and languages, should serve him: his dominion is an everlasting dominion, which shall not pass away, and his Kingdom that which shall not be destroyed. (Daniel 7:13-14 King James Version)

5 And from Jesus Christ, who is the faithful witness, and the first begotten of the dead, and the prince of the kings of the earth. Unto him, that loved us, and washed us from our sins in his own blood, 6 And hath made us kings and priests unto God and his Father; to him be glory and dominion for ever and ever. Amen. 7 Behold, he cometh with clouds; and every eye shall see him, and they also which pierced him: and all kindreds of the earth shall wail because of him. Even so, Amen. 8 I am Alpha and Omega, the beginning and the ending, saith the Lord, which is, and which was, and which is to come, the Almighty. (Revelation 1:5-8 King James Version)

3 And I heard a great voice out of heaven saying, Behold, the tabernacle of God is with men, and he will dwell with them, and they shall be his people, and God himself shall be with them, and be their God. (Revelation 21:3 King James Version)

True repentance is needed to begin your new journey into the Kingdom of Yah (God). If you fall, get up and start again. The enemy is going to send some of you diabolical devils to provoke you. Remember, the bigger the battle, the bigger the blessing. Your supernatural transition is coming. I'm excited just thinking about many of you flowing in your gifts of healing.

You will run into some that will say this is not the way. However, This is the way. It's free, and it will only cost you your obedience to follow Yah's lead. It's called your inheritance, and it's free.

Pray, seek the Lord, and he will direct your steps. Yah, and you are personalizing this journey together because the only one that knows your heart is the father. Encourage your brothers and sisters in Christ and pray for each other. (Ephesians 6:18 King James Version)

One thing we should clear up is that Yah (God) can hear your prayers, whether you are a believer or unbeliever, without a confirmed relationship with Christ. Our Father knows those who are searching for him, and he lays down foundations that will get you on the right path. He can't touch sin, but he sent his son Yahusha Ha Mashiach (Jesus Christ) to assist the unbeliever in a bridge back to his loving arms.

When I saw into the realm of the spirit, prayers captured in dark pits, the voices (sounds) seemed like a people in distress and fear. I saw a lady standing near the hole as if she was answering prayers. I came to the conclusion these are prayers of unbelievers and saints of Yah (God). Their captured fears fuel evil forces. Those four-footed beasts guarded this layer of darkness. Let us run our race in faith. We are human, and we have emotions; we feel pain. Encourage yourself in the Lord. (1 Samuel 30:6 King James Version)

The Lord is watching over his harvest of souls. It takes faith to pray. However, the hold-up has been one of demonic activity; many blessings and prayers are held hostage in the realm of the spirit. Do not always believe it's something you've done or did not do in life. That is a lie from the devil. The Lord does not cancel out answering prayers because you fall short. We are not perfect. We fall short and are not without sin. We are to repent and reapply our faith. Depression and discouragement can throw confidence off course and cause us to waiver. Some people start with belief, and when they don't see a quick enough response, they seek other alternatives or Gods. In spiritual warfare, it takes fasting and time to get prayers answered. (Daniel 10:10-13 King James Version)

33 But seek ye first the Kingdom of God and his righteousness, and all these things shall be added unto you. (Matthew 6:33 King James Version)

The Lord will deal with the children of disobedience who walk in wickedness. Yah has been more than merciful and gracious to call all too repentance. The Lord has one objective, souls for his kingdom. Let us have the mind of Christ and leave no room for the devil to inhabit our thoughts. (1 Corinthians 2:13-16 King James Version)

This journal will help you put all the missing parts of fragmented revelations together. The messages throughout the years became distorted.

Some words will appear repetitious; however, it is the balm of the Holy Spirit to direct and set you on course. (1 John 2:20 King James Version)

The Lord does not want his people walking in delusions. Proclaiming the title Chosen means nothing unless you know why you're a part of a chosen generation. You are the Church, and the Lord has not forgotten his promise to the Church. A path has been prepared for you to come through the realm of the spirit. Some of you might say that's creepy. It does sound a little scary when we start speaking about spiritual realms and moving supernaturally. However, you are the Bride of Christ, and that makes you a chosen generation a peculiar people. God is on the other side of that realm waiting for his Bride. He's in all his Glory! It's time to stretch your faith and believe for the unseen. The Body of Christ is made up of many cultures, different colors, and various economic backgrounds worldwide. Yah (God) and Yahusha Ha Mashiach (The Lord Jesus Christ) is the common factor that brings us to this season.

Whether you refer to him as Yah, Yahweh, Yahuah, The Most High, Elohim, Father, and Daddy, he knows when you are speaking to him as your creator. The Christ, Jesus Christ, The Son of Man, Yahusha Ha Mashiach, and The Messiah, we know we refer to our savior who died for our sins. Ruach Haqodesh, Holy Spirit, The Comforter, we speak the doctrinal names we know through tradition. If I say the I AM sent me, then that's who sent me that day for that purpose.

14 And God said unto Moses, I Am That I Am: and he said, Thus shalt thou say unto the children of Israel, I Am hath sent me unto you. (Exodus 3:14 King James Version)

Let there be no misunderstanding; the Lord is not going to fail you on the technicality of his name; he searches your heart. Moses was hidden in Pharaoh's house and Chosen. (Exodus 2:6,10 King James Version) Christ is our savior; he was our Chosen One and hidden in Egypt. (Matthew 2:13 King James Version) It's a title for big jobs when dealing with large numbers of people. Moses led the people out of Egypt's captivity; Christ died for the world. Along the way, we have had name changes not to offend anyone but for strategic warfare to set the captives free. You are entering into all truth through revelation knowledge. You are a Chosen generation! Where have you been hiding?

15 And ye shall leave your name for a curse unto my chosen: for the Lord God shall slay thee, and call his servants by another name:(Isaiah 65:15 King James Version)

It is the Father's Kingdom, and he is the Shepherd of his flock. There is only one way to the Father, and that's through the Son. Many are trying to get to the Father without going through the Son. It will not work. I pray that those on their journey would stop and begin again with true repentance. It is the blood of Christ that is the first stage of redemption. To enter into your inheritance, you must seek Yahusha, our Lord, and Savior the Christ. The Lord has gathered his holy prophets to begin the process of bringing his Church a Bride prepared without spot or blemish through the realm of the spirit. There are many believers (gentiles and the remnant) grafted into the Body of Christ who loves the Lord sincerely. They are willing to go to war for his namesake. The children of the Most High are eager to fight for their inheritance, healings, deliverance, and livelihood. There is no favoritism of who qualifies.

God is no respecter of person, and everyone who walks in the Demonstration of God's (Yah's) Power and Glory will become recipients of his promises. Follow his lead, and you will inherit his promises. Power and Glory will be to destroy the evil forces in the earthly realm, heal the sick, take back what the enemy has stolen, set the captives free, bring the Lord his new harvest of souls and take his remaining remnant home.

There is a massive harvest of souls to be won to Christ, for the Kingdom of Yah. The Lord wishes that none perish but that all should have everlasting life. Once you have conversed with the Lord, remember, do not judge the Church or fight against the Church. One of the most urgent assignments is to bring God's (Yah's) people into all truth.

Accountability is coming! If you are a Pastor or Leader, and you do not make it through the realm of the spirit into the presence of God (Yah), your ministry will fail. Your sheep will scatter. The Lord says, "Be Holy for I am Holy." Racism can't get into the Kingdom. Revenge can't get into the Kingdom. The Kingdom of God is within you, and you can't fake your way to the inheritance. The Lord has no desire to see his people struggle and be in chaos. Yah does not want his people on the sidelines, cheering on delusions and never arriving at their destination. He wants his children to be recipients of his promises.

This assignment is not about a Chosen few. The willingness to stand up and allow your flesh to die is your invitation into the Kingdom of God here on earth. You can't bring your bottle of wine, addictions, or spirits on this journey. Be sober and alert, and this is spiritual warfare. Only born-again Holy Ghost (Holy Spirit) filled believers can come through the realms of the spirit and enter his gates.

As a chosen generation, you have an assignment. Repent daily; worship is your warfare; cast down those imaginations as soon as they grab your attention, bring your thoughts under the obedience of Christ, and don't fight the Church! Walk-in Righteousness it's a requirement!

If you are sitting under a false apostle, just leave the dark foundation. Don't be taken away by false prophets who give your personal information like your name and address. Yah has blessed prophets with gifts; however, familiar spirits duplicate gifts. Satan is a copycat, and he comes as an Angel of light. (2 Corinthians 11:14 King James Version)

The gifts come without repentance; don't rely on them to show you the way. Unbelievers have gifts. Pick up your bible, read the scriptures, and allow the Lord to wake you up through revelation knowledge. I do believe Yah (God) always tells us first and then comes the confirmation. (Romans 11:29 King James Version) There will be no more going in circles generation after generation. Let today be your new beginning in the Lord (Yah). Ask Christ (Yahusha) to come into your heart and forgive you of your sins. If you fall (sin), repent, get up, get back in the race and begin again. Christ (Yahusha) is in the realms leading God's Army. The Father is on his Holy Hill on the other side of this earthly realm waiting for you. The path of the Lord is straight and prepared. (Mark 1:3 King James Version)

The Church was counting on a rapture, to escape the horrific chaos of the end times. We must be realistic because scripture teaches us that every man must die and then the judgment.

27 And as it is appointed unto men once to die, but after this the judgment: (Hebrews 9:27 King James Version)

Yah (God) will be coming back to earth and operating in you. Someone has to be on this earth to gather the Lord's harvest. He will not rapture you up and leave people to perish. He does not need a Bride in heaven; he just needs empty, clean vessels that can carry his Power and Glory through the earth. The enemy wants you to walk in confusion, with false results. I would not want my fate to be where I'm a tormented soul if I didn't make a rapture. If someone can't overcome their flesh addictions, then the ones operating in the demonstration of Yah's power will break those binding demonic yokes. The Bride of Christ's obedience is someone's answer and deliverance. You are the solution.

17 And I saw an angel standing in the sun; and he cried with a loud voice, saying to all the fowls that fly in the midst of heaven, Come and gather yourselves together unto the supper of the great God; 18 That ye may eat the flesh of kings, and the flesh of captains, and the flesh of mighty men, and the flesh of horses, and of them that sit on them, and the flesh of all men, both free and bond, both small and great. 19 And I saw the beast, and the kings of the earth, and their armies, gathered together to make war against him that sat on the horse, and against his army. 20 And the beast was taken, and with him the false prophet that wrought

miracles before him, with which he deceived them that had received the mark of the beast, and them that worshipped his image. These both were cast alive into a lake of fire burning with brimstone. 21 And the remnant were slain with the sword of him that sat upon the horse, which sword proceeded out of his mouth: and all the fowls were filled with their flesh. (Revelation 19:17-21 King James Version)

I hope these journal writings will help give you clearness on what the Lord has been doing behind the scenes to bring you to your destiny.

Revelation knowledge derives from The Lord (Yah). He chooses his vessels to whom he will deliver, his word, visions, dreams, experiences, or perhaps his audible or small still voice. The Lord has revealed his mysteries in different ways to his people. The Lord assigned me to reveal his will and anointed me with the revelation to direct his people into the promise of their destiny. Not a simulated future where you never arrive.

It will be your entrance into the spirit realm while leaving the dread of this earth behind and entering into the eternal presence of Yah (God) forever. (1 Thessalonians 4:17 King James Version)

If you have a dream or desire and just can't get to the next step, you've been spiritually high jacked of your blessings. If anyone tells you differently and says you are not doing enough, ask them to show you the way since they are doing plenty to receive. There are more chosen warriors, fighting for you, some behind enemy lines waiting for you to come up in righteousness in your war boots Bride of Christ.

Some have gone on to be with the Lord fighting for your promises and your children's inheritance. It's time to get moving today, take your assignment from Yah (God), and walk-in holiness and righteousness. We will enter the realm of the spirit in worship, not the way of the wicked in darkness. When it comes to the Lord's (Yah's) people, nothing is hidden, and we are the children of light. (1 Thessalonians 5:5, Ephesians 5:8 King James Version)

We, as believers, can look forward to the spiritual manifestation of (Yah). It should come as a norm for his people. The world assumes we are a crazy (peculiar) people because we believe in a God we cannot see by faith. (1 Peter 2:9 King James Version) We walk by faith, not by sight. (2 Corinthians 5:7 King James Version) We believe in a creator; we cannot see with our physical eyes.

Now you will strive and make a great effort to achieve what seems impossible to your natural senses because if your faith could touch Yah (God) to save you from your sins, then you have what it takes to cross over, receive your promises and inheritance.

We, the children of God, are to walk in the spirit and not fulfill the lust of the flesh. (Galatians 5:16 King James Version)

The fruit of the spirit consists of love, joy, peace, patience, kindness, goodness, faithfulness, gentleness, self-control, and is your road map to follow and enter into the glory of the living God. (Galatians 5:22-24 King James Version)

The fleshly desires of this world that would cause you to sin so easily are going to fall away as you enter and run the race with patience. Christ died for our sins, and we still have not conquered sin. On this journey, you will never return to old habits, bad attitudes, and sinful nature. (Romans 12:1-11 King James Version)

We will enter his presence with thanksgiving.

2 Let us come before his presence with thanksgiving, and make a joyful noise unto him with psalms. (Psalm 95:2 King James Version) We are an odd people who believe in the supernatural, and we walk by faith. Now faith is the substance of things hoped for, the evidence of things not seen. (Hebrews 11:1 King James Version)

FAN THE FIRES (PROPHECY)

As the fanners, fan the fire

I shall bring thee up to a higher place in me

As the fire rises, I shall bring thee up

Listen to my lead saith Lord You will not be disappointed

I shall raise thee up above the earth Again I say,

Listen to my lead saith the Lord

Let fanners come forth and fan the fires

Fires of song, fires of tongues

Fires of my warfare

Like a winnowing fan

I shall lift thee up in the wind

There I shall meet thee

and impart unto you

the demonstration of my power

Listen to my lead saith Lord

As the fires calm,

I shall rest you upon the earth

My fanners shall fan the fires

Like a wildfire

Listen to my Lead saith the Lord

My demonstration shall go forth

To the four corners of the earth

Listen to my lead saith the Lord

All Glory and Honor to the King of Kings and Lord of Lords

DRILLS (EASY TO READ REMINDERS)

DRILL #1 (YOU HAVE YOUR INSTRUCTIONS)

You've heard throughout recent years the scripture we are a chosen generation, or I am Chosen, perhaps in the jingle of a song. There's a war going on in the realm of the spirit. It's been going on thousands of years. However, we are the chosen generation that ends the war.

9 But ye are a chosen generation, a royal priesthood, an holy nation, a peculiar people; that ye should shew forth the praises of him who hath called you out of darkness into his marvelous light; (1 Peter 2:9 King James Version)

The Lord (Yah) wants those who love him to be encouraged, uplifted and inspired. He loves you, undeniably. He desires to bring you permanently into his presence. Our King can't bring you if you don't know where you are going and how to get there.

You've probably read the scripture enter at the straight gate. The passage means a belief that directs you into the extraordinary. It's not easy to get there because you can become deceived very quickly to go the wrong way that leads to destruction. It becomes complex when you have to believe something that goes against your natural way of thinking. However, the Lord does not want you to focus on this assignment being difficult. He wants you equipped with tools actually to get you in his presence permanently.

Enter ye in at the strait gate: for wide is the gate, and broad is the way, that leadeth to destruction, and many there be which go in there at: 14 Because strait is the gate, and narrow is the way, which leadeth unto life, and few there be that find it. (Matthew 7:13-14 King James Version)

The scripture says few find it. Well, who are the few? For many are called, but few are chosen. (Matthew 22:14 King James Version)

Everything derives from somewhere. This journey started over twenty years ago into the realm of the spirit. The Lord brought and taught me in the realm of the spirit. Which many refer to as the wilderness.

These drills are your crash course. The Lord has made a path for you to come into the realm of the spirit. Saint's you are going to need these skills to fight the adversary for your promise your survival. Many will say the battle belongs to the Lord, according to scripture. Yes, and you will be his battle-ax. (Jeremiah 51:20 King James Version) A body of believers fighting for the greater good for all humanity.

Saint's, your blessings are in the spirit realm. The Lord is going to equip you with his Power and Glory to handle the attacks against your livelihood. Remember, you have demonic forces in your earthly realm that will fight you day and night to hinder you from meeting the criteria of receiving your blessings. The wicked used a different door, but they have a different destination, and it's called the Lake of Fire.

It's not a good time for the devilish or evil forces, It's because God is on the other side of that realm waiting for you, his faithful people, His Bride. I know many people are waiting for the rapture because of wars, crime, poverty, death, and sickness. It does not make the earth appear favorable as a home. The Lord knows you are tired of quick-fix sermons that last an hour after service. Stop partaking in sources and materials that only prepare you for doomsday and does not speak life to your life.

The Body of Christ is the Lord's heartbeat. His people come in all beautiful colors. He searches the heart of man, and that's how he determines your relationship. No one can fake it into the Kingdom of God here on earth.

10 I the Lord search the heart, I try the reins, even to give every man according to his ways, and according to the fruit of his doings. (Jeremiah 17:10 King James Version)

Some people refer to him as Jesus Christ or Yahusha Ha Mashiach. Remember, the only way to the father is through the son Christ our Lord. Some people refer to him as God, the father, or Yahuah! Different names have yielded throughout the centuries. The Lord knew that there would be conflicts with his son's name. Our father is the name changer. (Isaiah 65:11 King James Version)

If you came through the Church, you were taught with the name Jesus Christ, and it works in power and brings salvation to the lost. It's Christianity that has failed the church. Corruption in the church makes a believer walk away. What the church was able to get away with under the guise of Christianity, it will not be able to enter into the Kingdom of Yah (God) with the same deception. The Lord is calling a Holy people who walk in integrity. Your past will not matter once you repent for your sins. Christ, your Lord and Savior (The Messiah) paid the price for your freedom. If you have fallen away, it's time to come back into the fold. Repent!

The Lord needs you, his people, to repent daily throughout the day. Your mind can get very busy thinking about the wrong thoughts and images. Try to focus on whatever is honest and pure. Demonic (evil) forces are assigned to sabotage you mentally to cause you to sin and walk in unbelief. Train your thoughts to cast down vain imaginations quickly.

If you think lust, evil, cast it down and repent, bring these thoughts under the obedience (submission) of Christ. We intake a lot of information into our minds. Having pure thoughts seems basically impossible, but it's doable. However, it is through the word of God that you can renew your mind. It will be your daily helper to assist you in combatting the demonic forces that use your soul as a playground. We do not know the hour he will come. Let us walk! (Matthew 24:36 King James Version)

Casting down imaginations, and every high thing that exalteth itself against the knowledge of God, and bringing into captivity every thought to the obedience of Christ; (2 Corinthians 10:5 King James Version)

When your mind begins to wonder anywhere unclean, unholy, or into a fairy-tale of vain imagining's, redirect your thoughts by casting down anything that exalts itself against the knowledge of God.

A lot of years have gone by, and still, the enemy has the church in bondage. The Lord has spoken to his leaders for years to turn from their wicked ways. Now It's time for the Lord to recover his sheep. Yah is not asking. Yahuah alone is the shepherd of his flock, and he is calling his sheep into his Kingdom. Numerous leaders have stepped up to their platforms and called the church to repentance. The church needs more direction. They need to know why they are repenting. The Body of Christ does not need another lie to cover the truth. They need to know the Lord has their promises.

Some writing's in this journal may sound familiar to some of the Lord's warriors, and for many, it will be the first time you've heard this message. Let there be no misunderstanding; God's warriors are not attacking the church. We are the Body of Christ and have our orders from the Lord. Do not fight the Church! We do not war against flesh and blood. This course correction will alleviate excuses. (Luke 14:16-24 King James version)

I wish I could tell you repentance is all that was needed to walk into your full inheritance. However, that is not the case. The church is out of God's order. It's not as if he did not know it would become polluted.

He has made provision in his Kingdom for his children to dissolve all flesh. (Romans 9:8-9 King James Version)

The Lord's Revelation knowledge gives you instructions to enter super-naturally into His Kingdom here on earth.

Worship is your warfare; it will be your biggest weapon that will assist you on this journey. Worship will deter all the evil forces in the realm of the spirit. Those tunes and lyrics permeate the atmosphere causing dark powers to scatter.

From the youngest to the oldest, you will come into your destiny in your ability to repent daily, worship, cast down imaginations, and do not return to former places of the flesh.

Drill #2 (WORSHIP IS YOUR WARFARE)

Drills are repetitive in military training and can become intensive when repeating exercises. It's important to follow the Lord's instructions and his lead. Yah has inducted you into his army. The Lord invited you, and you will come to his gathering prepared, referring to his Bride!

The Groom is ready to sanctify his Bride that he might present to himself a glorious Church without spot or blemish. You will become the host opening the gate who invites and receives new guests into the kingdom.

6 This is the generation of them that seek him that seek thy face, O Jacob. Selah. 7 Lift up your heads, O ye gates; and be ye lift up ye everlasting doors, and the King of glory shall come in. 8 Who is this King of glory? The Lord strong and mighty, the Lord mighty in battle.

9 Lift up your heads, O ye gates; even lift them up, ye everlasting doors; and the King of glory shall come in. 10 Who is this King of glory? The Lord of hosts, he is the King of glory. Selah. (Psalm 24:6- 10 King James Version)

14 That we henceforth be no more children, tossed to and fro, and carried about with every wind of doctrine, by the sleight of men, and cunning craftiness, whereby they lie in wait to deceive;

15 But speaking the truth in love, may grow up into him into in all things, which is the head, even Christ: (Ephesians 4:14-15 King James Version)

DRILL #3 (INTEGRITY)

Don't fight the Church! People have a different anointing, and the Lord will use them to their capacity! In the Body of Christ, saints can preach and sound differently. It does not mean they are fake! Win the race by holding your tongue. It's hard sometimes; however, calling names, dismissing people like as if they are insignificant definitely will not get you into the High Calling! It's a race, and you win by keeping your eyes on the prize, which is Yah! Worship is your warfare!

Walk-in integrity and respect your brothers and sisters in Christ. We are always to ask the Lord for a new anointing every day and walk in his grace. It's tremendously useful when breaking yokes, dealing with life struggles, overcoming challenges, and where wisdom is needed to combat the attacks on the battlefield of your mind. (Isaiah 10:27 King James Version)

21 Ye have heard that it was said of them of old time. Thou shalt not kill and whosoever shall say to his brother without a cause shall be in danger of the judgment: 22 But I say unto you, That whosoever is angry with his brother without a cause shall be in danger of the judgment: and whosoever shall say to his brother, Raca, shall be in danger of the council: but whosoever shall say, Thou fool, shall be in danger of hell fire. (Matthew 5:21-22 King James Version)

DRILL #4 SOULS FOR THE KINGDOM IS THE AGENDA

God loves his church, and the Lord is moving over the earth, watching over his harvest. His pride and joy. Pray, no weapon formed against his harvest shall prosper! Some people want Power and Glory to build personal thrones when it's really to set the captives free. My compassion is souls for his kingdom; because it's the Lord's compassion!

Anyone thinking of the harvest as a commodity get rich quick scheme is on the wrong path! The Lord God of Israel is in the business of saving lives even when they don't believe in Christ. That's what he's doing, keeping that harvest alive! That kid on drugs, Yah is keeping alive. The person who wants to commit suicide, he's keeping alive. The Lord wants his harvest! Let us put more prayers in the atmosphere for the loss of souls. Let there be no more premature deaths for our friends and families on this journey. Let us enter into his gates and get the power to heal the people we love through the Glory of Yah (God). (Matthew 9:35-38, Acts 16:31 King James Version)

Yah is about to uncover, uncloak, and expose people publicly who oppose his kingdom.

48 But and if that evil servant shall say in his heart, My lord delayeth his coming; 49 And shall begin to smite his fellow servants, and to eat and drink with the drunken; 50 The lord of that servant shall come in a day when he looketh not for him, and in an hour that he is not aware of, 51 And shall cut him asunder, and appoint him his portion with the hypocrites: there shall be weeping and gnashing of teeth. (Matthew 24:48-51 King James Version)

DRILL #5 CRASH COURSE

In this crash course, there will be a few changes in the way you usually perceive what you've been taught and what is true. For those saints who have received partial revelations throughout the years, I hope these writings I include will help fill in the missing gaps of revelation knowledge. God is Spirit, and those that worship Him must worship him in spirit and truth. (John 4:24 King James Version) Your instructions from the Lord are to repent daily (throughout the day). Do not fight the Church, and worship is your warfare. Cast down imaginations and every high thing that exalteth itself against the knowledge of God and bringing into captivity every thought to the obedience of Christ. (2 Corinthians 10:5 King James Version) If you have chosen to accept the Lord's invitation to the Marriage Supper Of The Lamb, do not fight the church or rally against them who are in opposition. Pray for peace and continue your journey with the Lord God of Israel (Yah).

The Lord is on the other side of this earthly realm, and he's moving over the earth. He's been there for years. He's in the earthquake and the floods. His power causes the earth to tremble. These are the beginning of the birth pains. (Matthew 24:8 King James Version)

The Church is about to give birth to the manifestation of God's Power and Glory. The Lord has come not to bring peace to the earth but a sword. (Matthew 10:34 King James Version)

Beloved, this would be a great time to take instruction and stay on a daily repentance. If my people will humble themselves and pray and seek my face and turn from their wicked ways, then will I hear from heaven, and I will forgive their sin and will heal their land. (2 Chronicles 7:14 King James Version)

Of course, this message is not only for the Church. The Lord came for his chosen people (His Remnant a small remaining quantity) who were stolen and scattered all over the earth, grafted in through his son Jesus Christ (Yahusha Ha Mashiach). (Jeremiah 23:3, Deuteronomy 4:27 King James Version)

Some sons and daughters of the remnant no longer attend churches or practice Christianity because they have come into their awakening. They have awakened to the truth that they are the bloodline of Abraham, the children of Jacob. Christianity led them to Christ (Yahusha Ha Mashiach), and it also drove them into all truth. God is not the author of confusion. (1 Corinthians 14:33 King James Version)

These writings are for the youngest to the oldest. The Lord is ready to bless his people. It's time to stop the madness of impatiently tapping feet and waiting on a promise to come to you via heaven. I'm not saying that blessings don't come from heaven into our earthly realm.

However, it was not the inheritance for this chosen generation who have committed their life to Christ (Yahusha Ha Mashiach). We, as believers, read the word and comprehend whatever version is presented to us in our generation. A lot of translation is way off base of the truth. We connect with the son of God (Christ) for our salvation and with the Holy Spirit (The Comforter) to connect to the throne room of Yah (The Creator, God). We worship, praise, and pray for a better life. We are thanking him for redeeming us from the darkness of this world.

We are instructed to pay offerings, sow seeds, and God will bless us financially. It all sounds great, and yet the majority of Yah's people are living paycheck to paycheck and many with no income worldwide. The Lord's people are sick and dying daily with unanswered prayers. The children of the Most High are waiting in expectancy and most never arriving at their physical healing and deliverance. If you're on medication, you are not healed and delivered. Medicine is a bandaid.

It's temporal. Drugs are not a healing from the Most High. It's a science created substitute to ease the pain. Why would the Lord give you medicine with side effects that would cause organ failure or another disease in the future? The Creator does not lift your hope to only bring you back to failure. The children of Yah have to decide this season if they want the true promises or to run their race in a circle and go nowhere spiritually in the Lord of Hosts.

The Lord is calling his people to a higher calling, and you just can't get there by using the old doctrines of men. You must come by way of revelation knowledge in Yah. The enemy came to deceive the whole earth. (Revelation 12:9 King James Version)

Let us not think in the future tense that we are going to be deceived, but in the past tense, we have already been fooled people of Yah (God).

We were born into the deception. We can't suddenly wake up go into freeze mode, regretting past mistakes of false teachings from the indoctrination and traditions of men. Yahs, Church, The Remnant, and The Warriors on the battlefield are waking up to the truth.

Doctrines were presented to you, and they lined up with the word. Some Scholars and Theologians showed research that was believable, decade after decade. Now those who seek accuracy are waking up to the truth.

Everything appeared legit in our teachings. However, a lot of deception was filtered into the belief system of Yah's people. All we hear is the end-times, the antichrist, and how we, the people of Yah (God), will be in anguish if we do not make the rapture. At least those left behind will be tormented with the unbelievers. The children are taken up because that would be too cruel to leave kids behind. No one would ever follow a doctrine or teaching that causes children to suffer. Many leaders are still teaching this old tradition and movie theater theology. Let us seek the Lord for our story instead of the media. Let us read the word and ask the Lord to reveal his mysteries and revelations. Do not just take my understanding and knowledge in this writing, people of Yah search by the spirit of truth. Praying, repenting, worshipping, studying, or read the scriptures in this journal, The Lord will bring you into all truth. It's your faith that will activate this revelation. (2 Timothy 2:15 King James Version)

The Lord loves his church, and he's not running out on the church. He's taking his grafted family whose redeemed by the blood of his son, into the promise of their inheritance.

If the Lord wishes that none should perish, then why are we trying to get raptured and leave people behind? What loyal child of the Most High or warrior would abandon a harvest of souls to escape the pains of this world? Souls for the kingdom is Yah's agenda. He comes as a thief. We would not know he has been here until we notice the goods are missing. He's coming, and he has his reward with him. We will meet him in the air. We are the goods. Power and Glory are the Prize.

The Prize is Yah! Don't forget he's coming with his reward and wrath. (Matthew 9:35-38, 1 Thessalonians 5:2-4,4:15-18, Revelation 22:12-14, Romans 1:18-32, 1 John 4:1 King James Version)

The Lord is on the other side of this realm, parallel to the earth. He's waiting on his Church, his Bride, to prepare and be without spot or blemish. When his Bride is ready, Yah's going to pull up the dead in Christ first. He's coming as a thief for his prepared virgin bride without spot or blemish. One taken one left, and he's going to meet you in the air pour into you a demonstration of his Power and Glory; come back to earth, operating his wrath destroying darkness and wickedness on the four corners of the earth. Not everyone will meet him in the air; however, the choice will be yours to prepare and follow his lead. You determine how much you love this corrupted world versus how much you desire to do the will of Yah (God). (Matthew 24:36-42 New King James Version)

You can't judge those who can't fight the darkness of oppressing spirits. However, a person with a mental disorder can enter the race. Worship is your warfare. Christ died for freedom and liberty for all, the sons and daughters of Yah. Even those who are tormented and considered outcasts. The Lord will reap his new harvest of souls through his called, faithful, and chosen servants who will be rewarded.

The word says we will be with the Lord forever. It means we will have walked in righteousness and holiness, and once his spirit fills us, the life of Yah (God) will inhabit our bodies. We will be with him forever spiritually on earth and in heaven. The Lord has an objective, souls for his kingdom, and this chosen generation is assigned to set the captives free.

DRILL #6 TIME FOR THE CHURCH TO ARMOR UP

Children of the Most High, if you feel lost, trust that the Lord is faithful to fulfill all His promises!

The voice of one crying in the wilderness, Prepare ye the way of the Lord, make his paths straight. (Mark 1:3 King James Version)

This scripture means clean up! It means the Church needs to prepare to meet the Lord ! He can't touch sin! It's time for the Church to become a virtuous bride without spot or blemish. Repent and come out of the darkness into his marvelous light!

When someone does something contrary to God, then it has to be undone! A lot of things in the realm of the spirit have been unaccomplished. The Lord is always moving and working for the advancement of his kingdom! Imagine trying to work around wickedness and not able to touch anything vile. His job is to keep you alive, and satan is trying to kill you. You are drinking, cussing, manipulating, lusting, walking in self-righteousness, and the enemy loves your playground of sin after accepting Christ as your savior. You're not repenting of new sins, and the father he cannot touch sin. Yah (God) has to create situations to bring you back on course to lead you to this place you are today.

Repent, and cleanup is the message for the church and Remnant! Anything not pleasing to Yah has to go! The baptism of the Holy Spirit is your comforter and a much-needed anointing for spiritual warfare!

The Kingdom of Yah (God) is not a transition of crossing the street from a Baptist church to a Pentecostal Church! It's not the changing of one doctrine to another doctrine! The Kingdom of Yah (God) is a spiritual transformation. Some saints will have to change their atmosphere of prayer and worship to avoid hindrances such as doubt and unbelief! Anything that causes your faith to become stagnated has to be removed.

A corrupted church can't enter into this transformation! Type and shadow, we say we are in the Kingdom of God! However, it's not the Kingdom of God where he dwells! Your flesh has to die to get into that realm of the spirit with Yah (God)! Satan knows the pure nature of Yah! The enemy was in heaven with Yah! The devil will hinder and assign evil forces to deter you (the church) from entering into his holiness! Why because you will become a vessel that can be used by Yah to destroy the kingdom of darkness! You will walk in supernatural power!

What's the point in being called a chosen generation a royal priesthood if you only have a title! That's like writing a book adding beautiful quotes. Sons and daughters of the Most High, you do not want to still be in the same position you were in last year or five years ago and profited nothing because you were on an emotional roller coaster ride. Hard-earned monies were sown into global ministries that only produce a facade! The Lord does not want you to think or believe it's all your fault, and you had no faith! You have had wicked oppositions; you could have never fought alone! Your blessings are now open to the earthly realm! Start marching in your race and take territory. The spiritual realms are on fire! You have the Holy Spirit; you can withstand the consuming fires of the Lord. Wickedness, dark powers can't get through those fires in the realm of the spirit.

Everything derives from somewhere! There's always a beginning and ending to every story! Never be afraid to ask how, when, where, and why! Know your opposition and know your team players! Our God is a proof producer! You've heard stories of how someone dies, and they see the light! They have an out of body experience, perhaps with God, angels, or family! They never want to come back, but then they are sent back! They end up in their recovery bed later, giving their testimony! You are going to have your out of body experience; then you are going to be sent back as a testimony in Power and Glory!

I didn't die in any experience going up or going over to his Holy Hill! I can testify it is real!

You are here on earth. You are alive for a purpose! To enter his Kingdom with him as your true shepherd and his undeniable power to do the greater works!

17 After that, we who are still alive and are left will be caught up together with them in the clouds to meet the Lord in the air. And so we will be with the Lord forever. 18. Therefore, encourage one another with these words. (1 Thessalonians 4:17-18 King James Version)

God is calling the church to repentance to pull them through the realm of the spirit!

If casting down imaginations bringing thoughts into captivity unto the obedience of Christ Jesus, repenting, surrendering all is doable for his army of prophets, then the Body of Christ (The Church) can fight good warfare and win!

The Lord gave platforms to his ministers to train his people. Elitists in the church need to repent. Time to stop taking partial revelations writing books that take the church nowhere! Those caught with their hand in the cookie jar in the realm of the spirit stealing and robbing saints, it's time to repent!

The church will need this demonstration of Yah's power and glory to destroy the works of false prophets. You don't want a familiar spirit giving out your name or address, and your house gets robbed a week later. Many can't see the evil force, but they have entered your earthly realm. That's one of the dangers of familiar spirits on the earth operating through the wicked!

The Lord wants to equip his church for warfare! Worship is your warfare! Each member in the Body of Christ worldwide can choose to armor up for his kingdom.

The only alternative is to be left behind and miss the manifestation of Yah coming in all His Glory!

The fear of the Lord is on the earth! Those who erred can come to true repentance!

If the Lord can take an army of prophets through realms (battlefields) from glory to glory, he can take a church (Body of Christ)! It's his Kingdom, and your spirit will meet him in the air! You will walk in Power and Glory, and you will have the firepower to defeat the enemy (on the earthly realm), and the church will possess the land and receive their inheritance! Yes, deliverance and healing will come! Get excited!

One thing to remember, God will not turn his New harvest over to a corrupted church! God is moving around this earth, watching over his new souls!

You are a Chosen generation! However, It does not mean you stay in the same state of sin and enjoy the inheritance of the Kingdom of God! Sin can't enter through the kingdom gate. There's no reward for wickedness and sin!

The Church needs to armor up and stay on a daily repentance. God is not a spirit of confusion, and this is not a new revelation; it's a revelation being fulfilled! I've seen two decades pass, and many leaders chose not to repent and line up with the will of Yah (God)! The Lord still built his army!

God has his Chosen people, who are the seed of Abraham's children of Jacob, many grafted into the vine through Christ! He's waking up their brothers and sisters. Some gentiles are Chosen warriors and chosen worshippers that battle against evil forces in the realm of the spirit.

Everyone in God's army has an assignment, and some wear many hats!

Many are in the marketplace, preparing to possess the land in business. He has called his faithful vessels, who are spiritual warriors, intercessors, and worshippers.

29 And Moses said unto him, Enviest thou for my sake? would God that all the Lord's people were prophets and that the Lord would put his spirit upon them! (Numbers 11:29 King James Version)

It's not too late, saints, to be a recipient of Yah's power, but you have to die to your flesh and line up those thoughts, and they obey Christ! Surrender all!

God has more than enough Power and Glory to light up this earth and pour out his Spirit on all flesh! Become a receiver.

Many leaders know God is on the other side of that realm! Delivering washed-up messages to his church will not suffice! Yah's not happy watching his church suffer and die!

A messenger can deliver the message; however, let there be no mistake in delivery! Remember, no Pastors, leaders, spouses, or parents can get you through the gate of the kingdom! Each member in the Body of Christ is responsible for their entrance into the Kingdom of Yah (God)! It's Your relationship with Yah and Yahusha Ha Mashiach! It's Yah who makes you an heir to inherit the kingdom. Many of you will have children, relatives who will be screaming and crying because it will be painful, leaving their flesh, contraband, and polluted Babylon behind. The atmosphere of transitioning will upset those comfort zones. (Acts 16:31 King James Version)

Righteousness and holiness mean the flesh is dying, and you are getting closer to your Creator. We are coming a different way to bring the church up through the realms. I will backtrack because everything derives from somewhere. If the Lord told us everything, in the beginning, our first response would most likely be, no way, nope or I'll pass.

I thought I was finished with darkness. Darkness covers the earth, and I figured I would go above the dark and stay up there where it's safe. I was doing this for so long that I thought I had to be finished on the lower earthly realm. I'm not coming back down for anyone; she is a pain in the neck. I say she because that entity darkness has female characteristics and an indescribable presence. She is like a force that protects evil over the earth. I even wrote it down delivered the message to prophets. I'm not coming back down. I gave them the revelation, some receptive and some not, some selfish. Then the Lord said his church has to come up. I thought to myself the church is coming, your holy prophets and apostles. Yah meant you his sons and daughters the Church!

On this journey, the church will have a full assignment. As you worship, you will begin to tear down strongholds and pray that the captives be set free. We have a worldwide epidemic on this earth of stealing children, teens, young adults, and women. The Lord pulled me into this realm of darkness. It was a place I kept envisioning years ago, and I didn't know where it was. I just knew I don't want to go there ever. Modern-day slavery, human and organ trafficking, is one of the most unimaginable and horrific acts humanity can commit upon another human being. Pakistan is the first country the Lord is calling to repent! Release the women and their children unharmed. The Lord says the ones you took on planes, put them back on planes and send them back to their homes and families intact. Release the rest to authorities and borders that they may be returned to their homelands. Yahuah declares if you harm any more of his children, Pakistan will never recover, Says the Lord God Of Israel.

The Church (Bride of Christ) will now intercede for stolen lives and setting the captives free.

It will become more intense for those who take on this assignment without fear. Did you ever wonder how someone could just disappear without a trace? Witches and warlocks do reenactments in the spirit to steal people and commit crimes. They use dark powers, such as rulers of darkness. How do I know? That's what God's Chosen Ones are assigned to do sometimes, go through realms, watch evil at work, and tear it all down, for our God is a consuming fire. They stifle authorities and bring confusion with evil forces. Some authorities can't stop what they can't see in the natural realm. If the enemy can send an oppressing spirit and throw us off course cleverly and subtly in our everyday lives, then evil can throw off law enforcement. Human trafficking is a black-market business, and the internet is the auction block for slavery and organ harvesting! The darkness that covers the earth protects this evil. Destroy all reenactments of the wicked in heaven and earth. Start sending up those prayers to release loved ones back to their families and homelands.

Break all curses and stipulations of curses placed on the souls (minds) of men. The oppressed are like dinner offerings for the wicked to obtain wealth. Evil forces do not work for free. They need to inhabit bodies if you want their help. Don't think mental illness is always a generational sickness. It's the reprobates that place the curses on the family bloodlines that are the problem.

You are going to war your way through these realms, uncloaking uncovering, and unveiling all darkness and wickedness. Fear them not therefore, for there is nothing covered that will not be revealed, and hidden that will not be known. (Luke 12:2, Matthew 10:26 King James Version)

You will now come up in the realm of the spirit and rule over the darkness. The Lord's glory shall be upon you!

2 For, behold, the darkness shall cover the earth, and gross darkness the people: but the Lord shall arise upon thee, and his glory shall be seen upon thee. (Isaiah 60:2 King James Version)

Run the race for the prize! We're almost at the finish line ! The wicked have been running the race; also, spiritual hijackers have been the Church's biggest opposition! Remember, they curse the church day and night in the realm of the spirit! Some will say you can't curse what God has already blessed. However, first, you have to get the blessing. Seek the Kingdom of God, and all things will be added to you. Now you have to seek instead of going in a circle of a possibility. Yes, the church has to armor up now! Clean out your houses. Do an Acts 19:19 get rid of horoscopes and anything which resembles the occult artifacts, materials with new age beliefs. Throw out videos with anything that represents the demonic. I got rid of emblems. I did not feel good about the star of David. Sometimes Yah is speaking, and we don't perceive. My first thoughts were it looks like a pentagram, then I thought everyone else had them on their prayer shawls. I could not find information on that star in history that makes it David's Star. If other cultures want a star, it's their choice. However, we are not taking any stars or artifacts through this realm to meet the King. (Job 33:14 King James Version)

Our God is a consuming fire! Pray and loose consuming fires and burn everything of wickedness in your path in the earthly realm, underworlds, underseas, depths, and bowels of hell and hiding places.

8 And five of you shall chase a hundred, and a hundred of you shall put ten thousand to flight: and your enemies shall fall before you by the sword. (Leviticus 26:8, Deuteronomy 32:30 King James Version)

About twenty years ago, I asked a woman of God; what did she think about God's Chosen? She replied a youth explained it to her, God's Chosen is like a basketball team. They play by all the rules, and they play to win!

We have heard there is strength in numbers, or many hands make light work. The Body of Christ coming together as the Bride of Christ as a team brings us into biblical prophecy.

4 And I heard the number of them which were sealed: and there were sealed an hundred and forty and four thousands of all the tribes of the children of Israel. 9 After this I beheld, and, lo, a great multitude, which no man could number, of all nations, and kindreds, and people, and tongues, stood before the throne, and before the Lamb, clothed with white robes, and palms in their hands; 14 And I said unto him, Sir, thou knowest. And he said to me, These are they which came out of great tribulation, and have washed their robes, and made them white in the blood of the Lamb. 15 Therefore are they before the throne of God, and serve him day and night in his temple: and he that sitteth on the throne shall dwell among them. 16 They shall hunger no more, neither thirst anymore; neither shall the sun light on them, nor any heat.17 For the Lamb which is in the midst of the throne shall feed them, and shall lead them unto living fountains of waters: and God shall wipe away all tears from their eyes. (Revelation 7:4.9, 14-17 King James Version)

Run the race! Yah (God) is your prize!

For I am not ashamed of the gospel of Christ: for it is the power of God unto salvation to everyone that believeth; to the Jew first, and also to the Greek. (Romans 1:16 King James Version)

Strive to enter in at the strait gate: for many, I say unto you, will seek to enter in, and shall not be able. (Luke 13:24 King James Version)

1 Verily, verily, I say unto you, He that entereth not by the door into the sheepfold, but climbeth up some other way, the same is a thief and a robber. 2 But he that entereth in by the door is the shepherd of the sheep. 3 To him, the porter openeth; and the sheep hear his voice: and he calleth his own sheep by name and leadeth them out. (John 10:1-3 King James Version)

14 If my people, which are called by my name, shall humble themselves, and pray, and seek my face, and turn from their wicked ways; then will I hear from heaven, and will forgive their sin, and will heal their land. (2 Chronicles 7:14 King James Version)

11 Put on the whole armor of God, that ye may be able to stand against the wiles of the devil. 12 For we wrestle not against flesh and blood, but against principalities, against powers, against the rulers of the darkness of this world, against spiritual wickedness in high places. 13 Wherefore take unto you the whole armor of God, that ye may be able to withstand in the evil day, and having done all, to stand. 14 Stand therefore, having your loins girt about with truth, and having on the breastplate of righteousness; 15 And your feet shod with the preparation of the gospel of peace; 16 Above all, taking the shield of faith, where-with ye shall be able to quench all the fiery darts of the wicked. 17 And take the helmet of salvation and the sword of the Spirit, which is the word of God: 18 Praying always with all prayer and supplication in the Spirit, and watching thereunto with all perseverance and supplication for all saints; 19 And for me, that utterance may be given unto me, that I may open my mouth boldly, to make known the mystery of the gospel, (Ephesians 6:11-20 King James Version)

Jesus Christ is Lord! Try every spirit!
Our God is a Consuming Fire!
Worship is your warfare!

DRILL #7 REALM OF CORRECTION

Yah is a God of love and compassion, and who he loves he corrects!

Before you start screaming, there's no condemnation in Christ! Scream, I will not sin against my God! Scream out, Lord, "I won't continue to fleece your sheep!" Scream Lord, I won't lie to your people and make these promises and base them on the word knowing that there is more to just receiving material possessions in this season!"

Woe unto the Pastors who bruise and scatter my sheep!

The Spirit Of Truth is here to prepare the Lord's people for the Kingdom of God! The Spirit Of Truth will not allow the Church to deceive the reality of entering into the Kingdom of God here on earth! (John 16:13 King James Version)

A chosen generation, a royal priesthood, is spoken as a generalization when the speaker does not know the revelation. Suggesting many happen to be in the right place at the right time!

A royal priesthood is much deeper than being at the right place, right time. It's a calling to holiness!

Call this the last season of deception to the Body of Christ! Because now there's new orders and instructions! The God of Israel will be leading his sheep! It's no secret to some that Yah (God) is on the other side of this earthly realm; he's waiting to deliver his people!

It's bad enough the wicked are in the realm of the spirit robbing Yah's people, but it's his people that break his heart with their participation!

Our orders are to go through the realms, get our weapons of warfare, and use power and glory to fight the enemy in the earthly realm! Yah's added orders were to pave (prepare) a way through the dominions for the Body of Christ to come up, and Yah (God) will equip them with their portion of Power for his Glory! Why? Because the Lord is not going to leave his people behind to suffer on earth. He's going to impart his spirit into his bride, who has no spot or blemish. Many people on earth have become so wicked that it has become difficult for the children of Yah (God) to discern. Sheep tend to follow their leaders; without ever thinking, leaders can fall and follow witches, warlocks, or the dark side. The darkness and deception are just that thick. When greed entered into the Church, some leaders learned the tactics of the wicked! Of course, this does not apply to all leaders! We've all heard leaders say the sheep are supposed to follow God because leaders can fall. However, you never listened to the Lord say, Woe unto my sheep who bruise and scatter my pastors. It does not change the fact that this is a learned behavior passed on for decades throughout the church! However, Yah (God) is taking over as your leadership to bring you into destiny! No more delays! Accountability is coming! (Matthew 24:24 King James Version)

God of Israel is bringing you into your inheritance!

Yah is a caring Father! His love is unconditional towards you! In his eyes, you've done nothing wrong! He's seen your despair and tears when you lost loved ones! He saw you give up when you sowed your seed and reaped no harvest! You thought it was your fault! You think it was something you did wrong! The Lord wants you to know it was nothing you did wrong! He saw you hold on to hope! He watched you lose hope!

The enemy comes to rob, kill, and destroy, and he uses anyone to destroy my people, says the Lord! Yes, my own were in the realms stealing from my sheep, hindering and manipulating in darkness! I will repay you for your losses and bless you, and your cup will run over!

My people, you will witness the supernatural. I will give you all that is needed to fight for freedom against the enemy!

The Lord called his Church leaders to repentance! Many did not answer; they continue to fleece his sheep!

The Lord speaks every language to his people all over the earth. He wants people in every nation to know he has not forgotten their love towards his son Christ Jesus (Yahusha Ha Mashiach).

Let those who are wicked still be wicked! They will never enter the kingdom of Yah!

Don't let anyone fool you, people of Yah, we could never have overcome this worldwide charade if it were not for the divine intervention of the Father (Yah) in heaven!

Years ago, in the realm of the spirit, I saw an entire realm of people of Asian descent! The domain was holding Asians hostage! Someone said Asians don't go to Heaven. Asians are not Christians! You don't have to be a Christian to go to heaven. You have to know the son Yahusha Ha Mashiach (Jesus Christ). This realm was so believable that you keep the thoughts in your mind after you left the domain. It's time to set all the captives free.

A while ago, I heard in the loudest audible voice in the realm of the spirit A man's voice angrily spoke SAVAGES! We all know that people of African descent were stereotyped with such harsh names. I believe I've found the Pharaoh in the realm of the spirit, which means he knows the remnant of God (Yah) is coming! If the remnant is gathered, then he knows the promises to the New and Glorious Church are coming to the Body of Christ. That's why there's a genocide in America and around the world to destroy black people. Murder and population control erases people. Who is the Pharaoh? It's an antichrist spirit that keeps Yah's people in bondage, poverty, lack, sickness, and under the curse of deception generation after generation.

We have to de-program ourselves from the traditions of men that we lose the battle on earth.

The wicked know more about what Yah is doing than his people! God is calling his people to repentance! It's time to wake up saints of the Most High!

Saul killed Christians, and the Lord forgave him. The Lord changed his name and made him a fisher of men! (Acts 9 King James Version)

Some of you, like Saul, are responsible for the loss of life worldwide! The Lord is calling you to repentance!

The Lord called his people to pick up their cross! He never called them to hide behind a cross, and go into the realm of the spirit, and do evil using their gifts!

The gifts come without repentance! (Romans 11:29 King James Version)

Familiar spirits are of satan! We are not to use our gifts to empower unclean spirits.

These last few months, I've heard ministers say something big is going to happen! Yet you knew part of the revelation for years! The worst thing you can do is not Repent! Repenting with void words and not sincerely meaning your words will cause you to be left out of his kingdom! Liars cannot enter into His Kingdom! (Revelation 3:14-22 King James Version)

I know a lot of you have a reason to fear Yah. You walked in your flesh a very long time in the church! It's been a flesh walk for all of us. One day in spirit the next day in the flesh, a constant battle. (Matthew 26:41 King James Version)

Yah is calling the Church to Righteousness!

Choose righteousness over wickedness!

The Lord wants his words to be clear to the Church. The Lord has not forgotten you! He will lead; you will follow! Some leaders have repented, and the enemy torments them with the past. Yah wants you to leave the darkness behind and walk in his forgiveness and righteousness.

The army of the Lord will fight for you until you are in the air to meet the Lord. Many are called; few are chosen to fight for you. Prepare yourself to be recipients of Yah's faithfulness!

Dying to your flesh, walking in love, and humility will begin your journey to become recipients of God's power and glory!

The Lord is calling those who dwell on the earth to repentance! He is going to pour out his Spirit on all flesh! Yah desires all of his children healed and for you to live on earth in peace! The enemy would have you as brothers killing brothers! The Lord says he will laugh at the enemy! (Psalm 2 King James Version)

You must seek Yah now! You can't fight these demonic forces alone; you need the Lord's (Yahusha Ha Mashiach) help! The Lord will fight for you until you are in the air.

The word says the very elect can be deceived! Why? Because you don't have a spirit of darkness! You have a spirit of light! (Matthew 24:24 King James Version)

False apostles and false prophets have to go! They send evil forces to monitor you. They use familiar spirits, and you need to give them a spiritual exit from this earthly realm. Whoever calls an entity (evil, darkness) into your physical atmosphere is crossing personal boundaries, and you have all authority to send it back to the sender.

If you don't verbally, with the power of your tongue, return these forces to the wicked, they will only keep sending you curses. Many people don't want to send them back because they have families that practice the occult. If a force is sent, it's not following you around for no reason. It's there to deter you from something valuable. (Zechariah 3:2, Jude 1:9, Matthew 4:3,4,10, Mark 1:23-26 King James Version)

We are to be loyal to the Lord Yah! Our family is in the Lord and the Body of Yahusha Ha Mashiach (Christ). Some might say, I can't send it back! Fear could be a factor or an indoctrinated tradition to love everyone and everything. Also, many have relatives who have not left the occult. They do not want curses on their family members.

Meanwhile, another child of the king is fighting for their life. Remember, Yah's (God's) ways are not our ways; his word says he's not coming to bring peace to the earth but a sword to divide families. If they are an enemy to the body of Christ, then they an opposition to Yah (God) (Matthew 10:34-40, Matthew 12:50 King James Version)

Many of you have anointing's that could shut down the forces of hell against the body of Christ, but you were never trained in spiritual warfare to open your mouth and speak against the darkness. Many family members can be saved from the corruption of this earth if faith would conquer fear. If you turned from your wicked ways, repented, prayed, and left your old behaviors behind. If you sought holiness and righteousness, captives would be set free. We cannot control family strays, who choose darkness. We can only pray that they come back into the sheepfold before it's too late. Whoever does the will of our Heavenly Father is family. These are the last days and perilous times men shall be lovers of pleasure more than lovers of God (Yah) having a form of godliness, but denying his power. (2 Timothy 3:1 King James Version) (Matthew 12:50, Proverbs 2 King James Version)

I am Yah's messenger. The Body of Christ must stand up and fight! Worship is your warfare! These are dangerous times, spiritually and physically! The Lord said he would pour out his Spirit on all flesh! This season would be an excellent time for you to receive that outpouring to combat darkness!

Hoorah, this is the end of the offering plate that Yah's people will pour into the false apostle's pockets. Important facts to remember! If a person supposedly a Prophet can tell your name and address and family members information in an audience, then what stops a crook, rapist, and kidnapper from visiting your house and committing a crime!

Imagine walking in a grocery store, and the person online next to you has a familiar spirit, and the spirit tells the person who's hosting the spirit you have money in your pocket and none in your handbag or wallet! That would be horrific to be robbed by a demon!

Your address is not needed in a church service! Watch for signs and wonders that seem awkward! Familiar spirits giving your location make your home a burglary spot and a death trap. The enemy comes to rob, kill, and destroy. There's always a cause and effect for everything! So there's no glory to God in disclosing personal information.

Sons and daughters of the Most High, this is the season to choose who you are going to believe Yah or another emotional sermon that lasts for a few hours or days! Will you accept the newest revelation of a scholar or theologian that only shows your demise and never arriving at the blessings of our Creator? False Prophets have to go! (Jeremiah 29:11 King James Version)

If you think you have problems now on earth, wait and see what you will have in a few years if you don't seek Yah (God) now in spirit and truth! It's time to armor up and prepare. (John 4:24 King James Version)

The Church needs the power to fight these diabolical devils and wickedness! Do not live life another day knowing that you can make a difference for yourself, family, friends, and the world.

Yah has plans to bless his people! Seek Yah! Walk-in forgiveness, let your flesh die daily, and repent daily! What the Church was able to manage in their flesh, they will not be able to manipulate in the Kingdom of Yah (God)!

The Kingdom of God is going to be a supernatural transition! Yah is going to take the foolish things to confound the wise! (1 Corinthians 1:7 King James Version)

Doubters will just have to sit and watch Yah (God) lead in his word that he created! (John 1:1 King James Version) Only the devil would orchestrate a lie that tells people to stay in sin, walk-in ungodliness, and prepare to be raptured up to greet a Creator that can't touch sin. This season choose whom you will serve. (Joshua 24:14-15 King James Version)

The Lord has his mysteries and secrets that he reveals to his prophets.

There's no need to solve a mystery that's already been revealed! It's time to move on to the next puzzle and revelation. (Amos 3:7 King James Version)

False leaders, there's no need to discredit Yah in his will or work by altering it to fit your next get rich scheme. The sons and daughters going through the realm of the spirit love the Lord God of Israel. They are all grafted into the vine through the shed blood of Yahusha Ha Mashiach (Jesus Christ).

No one will be able to fake righteousness and holiness in Yah's army, The Bride of Christ.

He's Yahusha Ha Mashiach, the son of Yah. You can spend your time debating names. He knows his people and the heart of his Bride (Church). The Lord is recruiting Eagles. (Psalm 7:9 King James Version)

Nothing will stop this move of Yah (God)!

Put the strong drink, wine, and contraband down and sober up that you may be counted worthy of hosting the Glory and Power of God in your temple. (1 Corinthians 6:19 King James Version) Walk-in Righteousness and repent!.

37 But as the days of Noah were, so shall also the coming of the Son of man be. 38 For as in the days that were before the flood they were eating and drinking, marrying and giving in marriage, until the day that Noe entered into the ark, 39 And knew not until the flood came and took them all away, so shall also the coming of the Son of man be. (Matthew 24:37-39 King James Version)

13 Brethren, I count not myself to have apprehended: but this one thing I do, forgetting those things which are behind, and reaching forth unto those things which are before,

14 I press toward the mark for the prize of the high calling of God in Christ Jesus. 15 Let us, therefore, as many as be perfect, be thus minded: and if in anything ye be otherwise minded, God shall reveal even this unto you. (Philippians 3:13-15 King James Version)

23 And this I do for the gospel's sake, that I might be partaker thereof with you. 24 Know ye not that they which run in a race run all, but one receiveth the prize? So run, that ye may obtain. 25 And every man that striveth for the mastery is temperate in all things. Now they do it to obtain a corruptible crown, but we, an incorruptible. 26 I therefore so run, not as uncertainly; so fight I, not as one that beateth the air: 27 But I keep under my body, and bring it into subjection: lest that by any means when I have preached to others, I myself should be a castaway. (1 Corinthians 9:23-27 King James Version)

PASSAGE

11/15/17

Around 2 PM

I saw into the realm of the spirit, a tide was coming in as my eyes adjusted to the darkness! The tide was coming in on my left. Then appeared a wide circular motion whirling back and forth in the darkness of the sky! It was as if it was trying to get my attention. My eyes became focused on this motion to look straight ahead. Then as far as I could see, I saw water with the tide coming in on my left! Then my focus was back in front of me, and I could see the tide coming in on my right. The tide was strange coming from the right because I then saw space between the tide, and I could see the beach floor (sand)! I thought, how can a tide come in, and dry land is between the tides. Then my eyes were focused on that circular motion again of what appeared to be a big midst that kept moving in the sky like zooming in and out and when I looked straight ahead, it was a wall of moving water on the left and a wall of moving water on the right as far as I could see. It was extremely dark. However, I could see the glistening of water and the entire floor of the beach. Then it was gone.

I then turned to my right and could see some activity in the realm of the spirit, a few people in the darkness moving around! It appeared to be some children playing outside, but it was extremely dark. I also saw the figure of a man moving around inside a house. The figure was pitch black. However, I could see and recognize images of furnishings as he moved around!

Around 3:30 PM while driving, I saw in the realm of the spirit again the wall of moving water on both sides! I ask the Lord what's the scripture? I heard "passage"!

11/16/17

This morning, I went to sleep at 5 AM and up at 7:00 AM. I heard a child speaking in the realm of the spirit! It sounded like they were giving information to someone. The child said," It looks like thousands of them. "Could that be an ocean? "Then the child said whose coughing? I could not tell if it was a boy or girl they were really young! Actually, I coughed! I'm getting over a really bad cold! The kid heard me!

The Lord has given us passage to come through that realm! The wicked appear to be using children where they can't get insight!

1 And the Lord spake unto Moses, saying,

2 Speak unto the children of Israel, that they turn and encamp before Pihahiroth, between Migdol and the sea, over against Baalzephon: before it shall ye encamp by the sea. 3 For Pharaoh will say of the children of Israel, They are entangled in the land, the wilderness hath shut them in. 4 And I will harden Pharaoh's heart, that he shall follow after them; and I will be honoured upon Pharaoh, and upon all his host; that the Egyptians may know that I am the Lord. And they did so.

5 And it was told the king of Egypt that the people fled: and the heart of Pharaoh and of his servants was turned against the people, and they said, Why have we done this, that we have let Israel go from serving us?

6 And he made ready his chariot, and took his people with him: 7 And he took six hundred chosen chariots, and all the chariots of Egypt, and captains over every one of them. 8 And the Lord hardened the heart of Pharaoh king of Egypt, and he pursued after the children of Israel: and the children of Israel went out with an high hand. 9 But the Egyptians

pursued after them, all the horses and chariots of Pharaoh, and his horsemen, and his army, and overtook them encamping by the sea, beside Pihahiroth, before Baalzephon.

10 And when Pharaoh drew nigh, the children of Israel lifted up their eyes, and, behold, the Egyptians marched after them; and they were sore afraid: and the children of Israel cried out unto the Lord.

11 And they said unto Moses, Because there were no graves in Egypt, hast thou taken us away to die in the wilderness? wherefore hast thou dealt thus with us, to carry us forth out of Egypt? 12 Is not this the word that we did tell thee in Egypt, saying, Let us alone, that we may serve the Egyptians? For it had been better for us to serve the Egyptians, than that we should die in the wilderness. 13 And Moses said unto the people, Fear ye not, stand still, and see the salvation of the Lord, which he will shew to you today: for the Egyptians whom ye have seen today, ye shall see them again no more forever. 14 The Lord shall fight for you, and ye shall hold your peace. 15 And the Lord said unto Moses, Wherefore criest thou unto me? speak unto the children of Israel, that they go forward: 16 But lift thou up thy rod, and stretch out thine hand over the sea, and divide it: and the children of Israel shall go on dry ground through the midst of the sea.

17 And I, behold, I will harden the hearts of the Egyptians, and they shall follow them: and I will get me honour upon Pharaoh, and upon all his host, upon his chariots, and upon his horsemen. 18 And the Egyptians shall know that I am the Lord, when I have gotten me honour upon Pharaoh, upon his chariots, and upon his horsemen. 19 And the angel of God, which went before the camp of Israel, removed and went behind them; and the pillar of the cloud went from before their face, and stood behind them: 20 And it came between the camp of the Egyptians and the camp of Israel; and it was a cloud and darkness to them, but it gave light by night to these: so that the one came not near the other all the night. 21 And Moses stretched out his hand over the sea; and the Lord caused the sea to go back by a strong east wind all that night, and made the sea dry land, and the waters were divided. 22 And the children of Israel went into the midst of the sea upon the dry ground: and the waters were a wall unto them on their right hand, and on their left. 23 And the Egyptians pursued, and went in after them to the midst of the sea, even all Pharaoh's horses, his chariots, and his horsemen. 24 And it came to

pass, that in the morning watch the Lord looked unto the host of the Egyptians through the pillar of fire and of the cloud, and troubled the host of the Egyptians, 25 And took off their chariot wheels, that they drave them heavily: so that the Egyptians said, Let us flee from the face of Israel; for the Lord fighteth for them against the Egyptians.

26 And the Lord said unto Moses, Stretch out thine hand over the sea, that the waters may come again upon the Egyptians, upon their chariots, and upon their horsemen. 27 And Moses stretched forth his hand over the sea, and the sea returned to his strength when the morning appeared; and the Egyptians fled against it; and the Lord overthrew the Egyptians in the midst of the sea. 28 And the waters returned, and covered the chariots, and the horsemen, and all the host of Pharaoh that came into the sea after them; there remained not so much as one of them. 29 But the children of Israel walked upon dry land in the midst of the sea; and the waters were a wall unto them on their right hand, and on their left. 30 Thus the Lord saved Israel that day out of the hand of the Egyptians; and Israel saw the Egyptians dead upon the sea shore. 31 And Israel saw that great work which the Lord did upon the Egyptians: and the people feared the Lord, and believed the Lord, and his servant Moses. (Exodus 14 King James Version)

12 For we wrestle not against flesh and blood, but against principalities, against powers, against the rulers of the darkness of this world, against spiritual wickedness in high places. 13 Wherefore take unto you the whole armor of God, that ye may be able to withstand in the

evil day, and having done all, to stand. Ephesians 6:12-13 King James Version)

Sons and daughters of the Most High, it's time to get moving towards destiny!

WORSHIP IS YOUR WARFARE!

Peace and Blessings

Love, Yah, and His Messenger

REFERENCES

Darby S (2015, May 29), "Blueprint for Our Destruction", Retrieved from https://www.youtube.com/watch?v=ENjG9nF8iM8

Goering, Sara, "Eugenics", The Stanford Encyclopedia of Philosophy (Fall 2014 Edition), Edward N. Zalta (ed.), https://plato.stanford.edu/archives/fall2014/entries/eugenics/ 2014, Metaphysics Research Lab, Stanford University

Windsor, R,1935- From Babylon To Timbuktu A History of Ancient Black Races including the Black Hebrews, BN Publishing

ABOUT THE AUTHOR

Sister Rose was ordained Reverend in 1997, under the Leadership of Grace of God Ministries. Sister Rose walks under an Apostolic Anointing and has been gifted as a prophetic scribe for over two decades. Yah has called Sister Rose to assist him in gathering his Holy Prophets who will stand for Righteousness and Holiness through revealed revelation knowledge on the information superhighway. She has dealt firsthand behind the scenes in this preparation process to deliver Yah's people from the oppression of the enemy. In her own experience, Sister Rose understands the cause and effect of life's daily struggles that her brothers and sisters in Christ endure from the onslaught of the enemy. Sister Rose has stood on the Holy Hill of the Creator and been commissioned by the Most High as a Chosen Warrior in the spirit realm to help cross over his Church the Bride of Christ and his remaining Remnant into their destiny. Sister Rose is the founder of Anointed One's Babes in Christ's Ministries. A loving Mom of three sons and six grandchildren, Sister Rose has a Bachelors in Communication Arts, and advocates for consumers with mental health disorders.

The Lord has mandated Sister Rose to build an End-time Refuge where he will gather his Chosen people back into their fold.

If this journal of Revelation Knowledge has blessed you, sow your seed into the Kingdom of Yah (God) here on earth and help Sister Rose fulfill the perfect will of Yah (God).

10 Thy kingdom come, Thy will be done in earth, as it is in heaven (Matthew 6:10 King James Version)

Send your emails to:
worshipisyourwarfare@gmail.com
Learn more:
www.yahandhismessenger.com
Sow your seeds to:
Cash App: $Endtimerefuge
paypal.me/chosenforglory
Venmo@Rose-Murphy-24

ROSE E. MURPHY

www.ingramcontent.com/pod-product-compliance
Lightning Source LLC
Chambersburg PA
CBHW021147090426
42740CB00008B/980